Gooseberry Patch

From our Kitchen to Yours

One-Pot Wonders

Table of Contents

Dedication

For every cook who needs an easy-to-fix, easy-to-clean-up meal!

•••••••••••••••••••••

Appreciation

Special thanks to every **Gooseberry Patch** friend who shared their very best one-pot wonders with us!

•••••••••••••••••••••

Gooseberry Patch
An imprint of Globe Pequot
246 Goose Lane • Guilford, CT 06437

www.gooseberrypatch.com
1•800•854•6673

Copyright © 2018, Gooseberry Patch
978-162093290-2

Welcome

Dear Readers,

Some days we need a hearty meal on the table in a hurry, and clean-up to be even quicker! So we've gathered over 300 mouthwatering one-dish meals in **One-Pot Wonders** cookbook to help on our very busiest days.

Whether you need a quick start to breakfast, lunch or dinner, these meals are all made in just one casserole dish, skillet, slow cooker or stove-top pot. Get a jump on your day with Breakfast Pizza or overnight slow-cooker Pumpkin Oatmeal. We've got soups and stews to warm you up, like Speedy Chicken Gumbo and Macaroni & Cheese Chowder. Dinner will be ready in no time at all with Fast & Fresh Asparagus Casserole and Oh-So-Easy Chicken & Veggies. And we didn't forget about dessert...Microwave Cherry Crisp Cobbler is ready in about 15 minutes!

Hectic days and busy nights don't have to mean fast food with **One-Pot Wonders.** Dinner's ready!

Jo Ann & Vickie

Chapter One

One-Pan Breakfasts

Wake up for breakfast! Whether you like to fix a hot and hearty meal to start your day, or grab a quick bite as you dash out the door, everyone likes a little taste of something yummy first thing in the morning. We've got time-saving make-ahead casseroles, show-stopper brunch tarts, slow-cooker oatmeal, pancakes, French toast, pizza, frittatas...so many great ways to start your day!

Layer 1/3 each of potatoes, bacon, onion, green pepper and cheese. Repeat layers 2 more times, ending with a layer of cheese. In a bowl, beat together eggs, milk, salt and pepper. Pour over mixture in slow cooker. Cover and cook on low setting for 8 to 9 hours.

Tracie Spencer, *Rogers, KY*

Hearty Breakfast Casserole

An easy-to-assemble make-ahead breakfast...perfect for busy mornings or when you have brunch guests!

Serves 12

6 to 8 bread slices
3-oz. pkg. ready-to-use bacon crumbles
1 lb. cooked ham, diced, or ground pork
   sausage, browned
2 c. shredded Cheddar cheese
10 eggs, beaten
1 c. milk
1 t. salt
1 t. pepper

Arrange bread slices in a single layer in a greased 13"x9" baking pan; top with bacon and ham or sausage. Sprinkle with cheese. Whisk together remaining ingredients. Pour egg mixture over top. Cover with aluminum foil and refrigerate overnight. Bake, covered, at 350 degrees for 45 minutes to one hour, until center is set.

Felice Jones, *Boise, ID*

Slow-Cooker Breakfast Casserole

This is a perfect recipe for busy mornings. You wake up, the house smells so good, and breakfast is ready as soon as you are.

Serves 8 to 10

32-oz. pkg. frozen diced potatoes
1 lb. bacon, diced and cooked
1 onion, diced
1 green pepper, diced
1/2 c. shredded Monterey Jack cheese
1 doz. eggs, beaten
1 c. milk
1 t. salt
1 t. pepper

Hearty Breakfast Casserole

Cheese & Chive Scrambled Eggs

Deborah Wells, *Broken Arrow, OK*

Cheese & Chive Scrambled Eggs

Paired with crisp bacon and hot biscuits, this is one dish we love so much, I've even served it for dinner!

Serves 2 to 3

6 eggs, beaten
1/4 t. lemon pepper
1 T. fresh chives, chopped
1/8 t. garlic salt
1 T. butter
1/3 c. shredded Colby Jack cheese
1/3 c. cream cheese, softened

In a bowl, combine eggs, pepper, chives and salt; set aside. Melt butter in a skillet over medium-low heat; add egg mixture. Stir to scramble, cooking until set. Remove from heat; stir in cheeses until melted.

April Jacobs, *Loveland, CO*

Grammy's Porridge

Raisins and apples seem to be made for each other, and in this homestyle porridge, they absolutely taste terrific together.

Makes 4 servings

1/4 c. cracked wheat, uncooked
3/4 c. long-cooking oats, uncooked
3 c. water
1/2 c. raisins
1/4 c. wheat germ
1/2 c. apple, peeled, cored and grated
Garnish: cinnamon, milk, honey

Combine all ingredients except garnish in a slow cooker. Cover and cook on low setting for 6 to 8 hours, or overnight. Spoon into serving bowls and serve with cinnamon, milk and honey.

～ Cook it Quick ～
Omelets, frittatas and cheesy scrambled eggs are easy to prepare for one or two...a perfect way to use up tasty tidbits from the fridge too.

Deborah Wells, *Broken Arrow, OK*

Huevos Rancheros to Go-Go

These are a favorite around my house...all the yummy ingredients for a great breakfast are wrapped up in a handy tortilla.

Serves 2 to 4

2 c. green tomatillo salsa
4 eggs
1-1/2 c. shredded Monterey Jack cheese
4 8-inch corn tortillas

Lightly coat a skillet with non-stick vegetable spray and place over medium heat. Pour salsa into skillet; bring to a simmer. With a spoon, make 4 wells in salsa and crack an egg into each well, taking care not to break the yolks. Reduce heat to low; cover and poach eggs for 3 minutes. Remove skillet from heat and top eggs with cheese. Transfer each egg with a scoop of salsa to a tortilla.

Amy Butcher, *Columbus, GA*

Sunrise Hashbrowns

Absolutely the best served with eggs sunny-side-up, crispy bacon and biscuits topped with honey butter.

Serves 4

28-oz. pkg. frozen diced potatoes
2 c. cooked ham, cubed
2-oz. jar diced pimentos, drained
10-3/4 oz. can Cheddar cheese soup
3/4 c. milk
1/4 t. pepper

In a slow cooker, combine potatoes, ham and pimentos. In a bowl, combine soup, milk and pepper; pour over potato mixture. Cover and cook on low setting for 6 to 8 hours.

∼ Cook it Quick ∼

For speedy recipe prep, store all the breakfast foods on one shelf in the refrigerator and one shelf in your cupboard.

Huevos Rancheros to Go-Go

Pigs in the Clover

Cathy Nign, *Temple City, CA*

Pigs in the Clover

My Norwegian mother-in-law gave me this recipe. She told me this was a dish she ate while growing up.

Serves 4 to 6

14-3/4 oz. can creamed corn
2 to 3 potatoes, peeled, boiled and cubed
salt and pepper to taste
8 pork breakfast sausage links, browned

Pour creamed corn into a greased 8"x8" baking pan. Place potatoes over corn; sprinkle with salt and pepper. Arrange sausage links on top. Cover with aluminum foil. Bake at 350 degrees for 30 minutes, or until bubbly.

Chad Rutan, *Gooseberry Patch*

Green Eggs & Ham

These are so good, I will eat them on a plane, on a train, on a boat, in a coat...anywhere, anytime!

Serves one to 2

2 T. butter
1/2 c. fresh spinach
1 green onion, chopped
1/4 c. deli smoked ham, diced
3 eggs, beaten
2 T. pesto sauce
salt and pepper to taste

Melt butter in a skillet over medium heat. Cook spinach, green onion and ham in butter until warmed through and spinach is wilted, about 3 minutes. Add eggs to spinach mixture and cook until eggs start to set; stir in pesto, salt and pepper. Continue cooking until eggs reach desired doneness.

Elizabeth Blackstone, *Racine, WI*

Berry Bog Oatmeal

Cranberries and a touch of honey turn ordinary oatmeal into a breakfast the whole family looks forward to.

Serves 4

1 c. steel-cut oats, uncooked
1 c. sweetened, dried cranberries
1 c. chopped dates
4 c. water
1/2 c. half-and-half
2 T. honey

Combine oats, cranberries, dates and water in a greased slow cooker. Cover and cook on low setting for 6 to 8 hours. Stir in half-and-half and honey.

Flavor Booster
·············· ✳ ··············

Fresh fruit is perfect pairing with early-morning recipes. Set out plump strawberries, juicy oranges, peach slices and fresh berries to enjoy alongside favorite breakfast dishes. Serve with a bowl of sugar or cream alongside...just to make it extra special.

Beth Kramer, *Port Saint Lucie, FL*

Blueberry Breakfast Cake

If you like moist blueberry muffins, you're gonna love this cake.

Serves 6

6-1/2 oz. pkg. blueberry muffin mix, divided
1/4 c. milk
1 egg, beaten
1/8 t. cinnamon

Reserve 1/4 cup muffin mix for use in another recipe. Spray a slow cooker with non-stick vegetable spray. Stir together remaining muffin mix, milk, egg and cinnamon just until combined; spoon into slow cooker, spreading evenly. Cover top of slow cooker with 6 to 8 paper towels to absorb condensation. Cover and cook on high setting for one hour. Turn off slow cooker and let stand for 10 minutes. Loosen edges of cake with a knife. Place a plate on top of slow cooker; invert to remove. Place another plate on top of cake and invert again. Slice into wedges.

Connie Hilty, *Pearland, TX*

Breakfast Pizza

Is there anything better than pizza for breakfast?

Serves 2 to 4

11-oz. tube refrigerated thin-crust pizza dough
14-oz. can pizza sauce
16-oz. container ricotta cheese
1/4 c. fresh oregano, chopped
favorite pizza toppings
4 eggs
salt and pepper to taste

Roll out dough into a 13-inch by 9-inch rectangle; transfer to a greased rimmed baking sheet. Spread pizza sauce on dough, leaving a 1/2-inch border. Top with cheese, oregano and other pizza toppings. Bake at 500 degrees for 4 to 5 minutes, or until crust begins to turn golden. Crack each egg into a small bowl and slip onto pizza, being careful not to break the yolks. Bake for another 5 minutes, until eggs are done as desired.

Breakfast Pizza

Mel Chencharick, *Julian, PA*

Lazy Man's Pancakes

This is great when you're pressed for time. No more standing at the stove for an hour flipping and frying... just mix and pop in the oven.

Serves 5 to 6

3 T. butter
6 eggs, beaten
1-1/2 c. milk
1-1/2 c. all-purpose flour
3/4 t. salt
Optional: chopped walnuts, maple syrup

Melt butter in a 13"x9" baking pan placed in a 425-degree oven. Meanwhile, in a bowl, combine eggs, milk, flour and salt; beat well. Slowly pour mixture into buttered pan. Bake at 425 degrees for 20 to 25 minutes, until top is golden. Cut into squares; serve topped with nuts and syrup, if desired.

Kim Faulkner, *Columbus, OH*

Apple Pie Bread Pudding

We made apple pie jam last September, so we thought, why not try pie filling in a bread pudding recipe? I'm glad we did...it's a scrumptious breakfast treat.

Makes 6 servings

3 eggs, beaten
2 c. milk
1/2 c. sugar
21-oz. can apple pie filling
6-1/2 c. cinnamon-raisin bread, cubed
Optional: whipped cream

In a large bowl, whisk together eggs, milk and sugar. Gently stir in pie filling and bread cubes; pour mixture into a lightly greased slow cooker. Cover and cook on low setting for 3 hours, or until a knife inserted near center comes out clean. Remove crock from cooker, if possible, or turn off cooker. Let stand, uncovered, for 30 to 45 minutes to cool slightly before serving. Spoon bread pudding into serving bowls. If desired, top each serving with a dollop of whipped cream.

Lazy Man's Pancakes

Apple Breakfast Cobbler

Debi Gilpin, *Sharpsburg, GA*

Apple Breakfast Cobbler

What a fabulous slow-cooker treat to wake up to on a chilly winter morning!

Serves 4

4 apples, peeled, cored and sliced
1/4 c. honey
1 t. cinnamon
2 T. butter, melted
2 c. granola cereal
Garnish: milk or cream

Place apples in a slow cooker sprayed with non-stick vegetable spray. In a bowl, combine remaining ingredients except garnish; sprinkle over apples. Cover and cook on low setting for 7 to 9 hours, or on high setting for 3 to 4 hours. Garnish with milk or cream.

Shannon James, *Georgetown, KY*

Pumpkin Oatmeal

I have 4 small children, so my love for cooking can only come out late at night once they have gone to bed. This is always a favorite in the fall and around the holidays. Who doesn't love waking up to the sweet and spicy aroma of pumpkin baking?

Makes 6 to 8 servings

2 c. long-cooking oats, uncooked
1 c. canned pumpkin pie filling
2 c. milk
2 c. water
1/4 c. butter
1/2 t. salt
Garnish: whipped cream, maple syrup

Mix together all ingredients except garnish in a lightly greased slow cooker. Cover and cook on low setting for 6 to 8 hours. Serve with a dollop of whipped cream or a drizzle of maple syrup.

Vickie, *Gooseberry Patch*

Farmers' Market Omelet

I love visiting the farmers' market bright & early on Saturday mornings...a terrific way to begin the day!

Serves 1

1 t. olive oil
1 slice bacon, diced
2 T. onion, chopped
2 T. zucchini, diced
5 cherry tomatoes, quartered
1/2 t. fresh thyme, minced
3 eggs, beaten
1/4 c. fontina cheese, shredded

Heat oil in a skillet over medium-high heat. Add bacon and onion; cook and stir until bacon is crisp and onion is tender. Add zucchini, tomatoes and thyme. Allow to cook until zucchini is soft and juice from tomatoes has slightly evaporated. Lower heat to medium and stir in eggs. Cook, lifting edges to allow uncooked egg to flow underneath. When eggs are almost fully cooked, sprinkle with cheese and fold over.

Penny Sherman, *Cumming, GA*

Grits with Gusto

If you like breakfast a little spicy... sprinkle warm grits with a tablespoon or two of shredded cheese and dollop a spoonful of hot salsa right in the middle.

Makes 6 servings

2 c. long-cooking grits, uncooked
6 c. water
4-oz. can chopped green chiles
1 jalapeño pepper, seeded and finely chopped
1/8 t. cayenne pepper
1 t. salt
Optional: 1/2 t. paprika, 1/2 t. chili powder
Garnish: butter, salt and pepper

Combine all ingredients except garnish in a lightly greased slow cooker; mix well. Cover and cook on low setting for about 8 hours. Stir after first hour of cooking; stir well before serving. Serve with butter, salt and pepper.

Farmers' Market Omelet

Orange-Cinnamon French Toast

Debra Fleischacker, *Aurora, CO*

Orange-Cinnamon French Toast

Good recipes always get passed along, as this one will!

Serves 3 to 4

2 to 4 T. butter, melted
2 T. honey
1/2 t. cinnamon
3 eggs, beaten
1/2 c. frozen orange juice concentrate, partially
  thawed
1/8 t. salt
6 slices French bread

Combine butter, honey and cinnamon together in a 13"x9" baking pan and set aside. Blend eggs, orange juice and salt together. Dip bread slices into egg mixture, coating both sides. Arrange dipped bread slices in baking pan. Bake, uncovered, at 400 degrees for 15 to 20 minutes, until golden.

Lora Montgomery, *Delaware, OH*

Eggs with Cheddar & Bacon

For a twist, try maple-flavored bacon or even pepper bacon in this recipe.

Makes 6 to 8 servings

3 to 4 c. crusty bread, diced
1/2 lb. bacon, crisply cooked, crumbled and
  1 T. drippings reserved
Optional: 2 to 3 c. favorite vegetables, chopped
8 eggs, beaten
1/2 c. milk
1 c. shredded Cheddar cheese
salt and pepper to taste

Place bread in a lightly greased slow cooker. If using vegetables, heat reserved drippings in a large skillet over medium heat. Sauté vegetables, tossing to coat. Stir bacon and vegetables into bread. Whisk together eggs and milk in a medium bowl; stir in cheese, salt and pepper. Pour over bread mixture. Cover and cook on low setting for 3 to 3-1/2 hours, until eggs are set.

~ *Cook it Quick* ~

Frying up a skillet of bacon for breakfast? If there's no spatter guard handy, a large sieve can do the job...just place it face-down over the skillet.

Linda Bonwill, *Englewood, FL*

Spinach & Tomato French Toast

A healthier way to make French toast...plus, it looks so pretty!

Serves 4

3 eggs, beaten
salt and pepper to taste
8 slices Italian bread
4 c. fresh spinach, torn
2 tomatoes, sliced
Garnish: grated Parmesan cheese

In a bowl, beat eggs with salt and pepper. Dip bread slices into egg mixture. Place in a lightly greased skillet over medium heat; cook one side until lightly golden. Place fresh spinach and 2 slices of tomato onto each slice, pressing lightly to secure. Flip and briefly cook on other side until golden.

Lynda Robson, *Boston, MA*

Early Bird Oatmeal

You'll never have "plain" oatmeal again!

Serves 4 to 6

3 c. long-cooking oats, uncooked
3/4 c. powdered sugar
1/4 t. salt
21-oz. can cherry pie filling
6 c. water
1 t. almond extract

Combine oats, powdered sugar and salt in a large bowl; pour into a slow cooker that has been sprayed with non-stick vegetable spray. Add remaining ingredients; stir until combined. Cover and cook on low setting for 6 to 8 hours.

Flavor Booster

·············· ✳ ··············

Homemade fruit jam isn't just for spreading on bread. Stir a spoonful into warm breakfast oatmeal...yum!

Spinach & Tomato French Toast

Mamaw's Breakfast Cobbler

Virginia Watson, *Scranton, PA*

Grandma's Warm Breakfast Fruit

Keep this warm for brunch in a mini slow cooker.

Serves 6 to 8

3 apples, peeled, cored and thickly sliced
1 orange, peeled and sectioned
3/4 c. raisins
1/2 c. dried plums, chopped
3 c. plus 3 T. water, divided
1/2 c. sugar
1/2 t. cinnamon
2 T. cornstarch
Garnish: granola

Combine fruit and 3 cups water in a saucepan over medium heat. Bring to a boil; reduce heat and simmer for 10 minutes. Stir in sugar and cinnamon. In a small bowl, mix together cornstarch and remaining water; stir into fruit mixture. Bring to a boil, stirring constantly; cook and stir for 2 minutes. Spoon into bowls; top with granola to serve.

Melanie Lowe, *Dover, DE*

Mamaw's Breakfast Cobbler

My grandma makes this breakfast treat whenever we visit her at the farm. It's always a wonderful time... gathering eggs, riding horses and staying up way past bedtime!

Serves 4

2 c. tart apples, peeled, cored and sliced
2 c. granola cereal
1 t. cinnamon
1/4 c. honey
2 T. butter, melted

Combine apples, cereal and cinnamon in a lightly greased slow cooker and mix well. Stir together honey and butter; drizzle over apple mixture. Blend gently. Cover and cook on low setting for 8 hours, until apples are tender.

Flavor Booster

················ ✳ ················

Add a pinch of lemon, lime or orange zest to your morning oatmeal for fresh, sunny flavor!

Lita Hardy, *Santa Cruz, CA*

Best Brunch Casserole

My family & friends have been enjoying this dish for over 30 years!

Serves 8

4 c. croutons
2 c. shredded Cheddar cheese
8 eggs, beaten
4 c. milk
1 t. salt
1 t. pepper
2 t. mustard
1 T. dried, minced onion
6 slices bacon, crisply cooked and crumbled

Spread croutons in a greased 13"x9" baking pan; sprinkle with cheese and set aside. In a bowl, whisk together remaining ingredients except bacon; pour over cheese. Sprinkle bacon on top. Bake, uncovered, at 325 degrees for 55 to 60 minutes, until set.

Samantha Sparks, *Madison, WI*

Mom's Rice Porridge

You can use either medium-grain or short-grain rice in this recipe.

Serves 2 to 4

1 c. long-cooking rice, uncooked
2 c. water
1-1/2 c. evaporated milk
1/2 t. salt
1/2 c. raisins

Combine all the ingredients in a slow cooker. Cover and cook on low setting for 6 to 8 hours, or overnight.

~ *Cook it Quick* ~

Having friends over for breakfast or brunch? Set the table the night before...one less thing to think about in the morning!

Best Brunch Casserole

Hashbrown Quiche

Sonya Labbe, *Santa Monica, CA*

Hashbrown Quiche

The crust of this quiche is made with frozen hashbrowns. It is always a hit at family potlucks and brunches.

Serves 4 to 6

3 c. frozen shredded hashbrowns, thawed
1/4 c. butter, melted
3 eggs, beaten
1 c. half-and-half
3/4 c. cooked ham, diced
1/2 c. green onions, chopped
1 c. shredded Cheddar cheese
salt and pepper to taste

In an ungreased 9" pie plate, combine hashbrowns and butter. Press hashbrowns into the bottom and up the sides of the pie plate. Bake at 450 degrees for 20 to 25 minutes, until golden and crisp. Remove from oven and cool slightly. Meanwhile, combine remaining ingredients in a bowl. Pour mixture over hashbrowns. Lower oven temperature to 350 degrees; bake for 30 minutes, or until quiche is golden and set.

Patti Suk, *Rochester, MN*

Eggs Olé

Set out plenty of sour cream and salsa for spooning on top...tasty!

Serves 12

3 4-oz. cans diced green chiles
16-oz. pkg. Monterey Jack cheese, sliced
1 doz. eggs, beaten
2 c. sour cream
salt and pepper to taste

Spoon chiles into a greased 13"x9" baking pan; top with cheese. Set aside. Beat eggs and sour cream together; pour over cheese. Sprinkle with salt and pepper; bake at 375 degrees for 30 to 40 minutes.

Jill Ross, *Pickerington, OH*

Breezy Brunch Skillet

This one-skillet meal is a snap to toss together, and the results are scrumptious. I'll even cook this up for dinner, it's so good!

Serves 4

6 slices bacon, diced
6 c. frozen diced potatoes
3/4 c. green pepper, chopped
1/2 c. onion, chopped
1 t. salt
1/4 t. pepper
4 eggs
1/2 c. shredded Cheddar cheese

In a large skillet over medium heat, cook bacon until crisp. Drain and set aside, reserving 2 tablespoons drippings. In the same skillet, add potatoes, green pepper, onion, salt and pepper to drippings. Cook and stir for 2 minutes. Cover and cook for about 15 minutes, stirring occasionally, until potatoes are golden and tender. With a spoon, make 4 wells in potato mixture. Crack one egg into each well, taking care not to break the yolks. Cover and cook on low heat for 8 to 10 minutes, until eggs are completely set. Sprinkle with cheese and bacon.

Jane Skillin, *Montclair, NJ*

3-Cheese Western Omelet

A classic omelet baked to cheesy perfection.

Makes 6 servings

3/4 c. mild salsa
1 c. artichoke hearts, chopped
1/4 c. grated Parmesan cheese
1 c. shredded Monterey Jack cheese
1 c. shredded Cheddar cheese
6 eggs, beaten
1 c. sour cream

Spread salsa in the bottom of a greased 10" pie plate. Sprinkle artichokes over salsa; top with cheeses. Set aside. Blend eggs and sour cream together; spread over cheeses. Bake at 350 degrees for 30 minutes, or until set. Cut into wedges to serve.

Breezy Brunch Skillet

Easy Breakfast Squares

Vicki Hirsch, *Platteville, WI*

Easy Breakfast Squares

This overnight dish is filled with all your breakfast favorites!

Serves 6 to 8

24-oz. pkg. frozen shredded hashbrowns
1-1/2 c. shredded mozzarella cheese
1-1/2 c. shredded Cheddar cheese
1 onion, diced
2 c. cooked ham, diced
salt and pepper to taste
3 eggs, beaten
1 c. milk

In a lightly greased 13"x9" baking pan, layer hashbrowns, cheeses, onion and ham; season with salt and pepper. Set aside. In a bowl, beat together eggs and milk; pour over ham. Cover; refrigerate 8 hours to overnight. Uncover; bake at 350 degrees for 45 minutes. Cut into squares to serve.

Flavor Booster

∗

A cup of herbal tea is perfect with breakfast recipes. Instead of sweetening with sugar, drop in one or 2 old-fashioned lemon drops.

Olive Herzberg, *Lomita, CA*

Mexican Brunch Casserole

This is a great brunch dish...it's got yummy Mexican flavors that are sure to have you coming back for seconds.

Serves 3 to 4

2 4-oz. cans whole green chiles, drained
2 to 3 tomatoes, chopped
2 c. shredded Colby Jack cheese
1 c. biscuit baking mix
3 eggs, beaten
1 c. milk
1/2 t. salt

In a lightly greased 8"x8" baking pan, layer chiles, tomatoes and cheese. Beat together remaining ingredients and spoon over cheese. Bake, uncovered, at 375 degrees for 30 to 35 minutes, until set.

Melanie Lowe, *Dover, DE*

Milk & Honey Couscous

This quick-to-fix breakfast is perfect for those chilly mornings when you need something to fill you up and keep you warm.

Serves 6

2 c. milk
2 T. honey
1 T. cinnamon
2 c. couscous, uncooked
1/3 c. dried apricots, chopped
1/3 c. raisins
1/2 c. slivered almonds

Combine milk, honey and cinnamon in a saucepan over medium heat. Bring to a boil; stir in couscous. Remove from heat; cover and let stand for 5 minutes. Fold in remaining ingredients.

Lynda McCormick, *Burkburnett, TX*

Rise & Shine Breakfast Soufflé

A quick-to-fix overnight casserole.

Serves 8 to 10

1 lb. ground pork sausage, browned and drained
9 eggs, beaten
3-1/2 c. milk
1 t. mustard
6 to 8 slices bread, cubed
1-1/2 c. shredded Cheddar cheese
10-3/4 oz. can cream of mushroom soup
4 c. corn flake cereal, crushed
1/2 c. butter, melted

Mix sausage, eggs, milk, mustard, bread, cheese and soup in a bowl; spoon into a greased 13"x9" baking pan. Cover; refrigerate overnight. Remove from refrigerator 30 minutes before baking; set aside. Combine cereal and butter; sprinkle over egg mixture. Bake at 350 degrees for one hour.

Milk & Honey Couscous

Blueberry Oatmeal Crisp

Amy Bastian, *Mifflinburg, PA*

Blueberry Oatmeal Crisp

This crisp is perfect on a brisk fall morning. Paired with some hot tea, it'll keep you warm and full all morning!

Makes 6 to 8 servings

4 c. blueberries
1 c. all-purpose flour, divided
3/4 c. brown sugar, packed
3/4 c. long-cooking oats, uncooked
1/2 t. cinnamon
1/4 t. nutmeg
5 to 6 T. butter

Combine blueberries with 1/4 cup flour in a greased 11"x7" baking pan; mix thoroughly. In a bowl, combine remaining flour and other ingredients except butter. Cut in butter until coarse crumbs form; sprinkle over blueberries. Bake at 350 degrees for 25 minutes, or until top is golden and blueberries are bubbly.

Corinne Ficek, *Normal, IL*

Finnish Pancakes

A moist, custard-like treat that can be served with syrup, jelly or honey.

Serves 4

3 T. butter, melted
4 eggs
2 c. milk
1 c. all-purpose flour
1/8 t. salt
1 T. sugar
1 t. vanilla extract

Melt butter in a 13"x9" baking pan in the oven at 400 degrees; set aside. Place eggs in a blender; blend well. Add milk, flour, salt, sugar and vanilla; blend thoroughly. Pour into pan; bake at 400 degrees for 35 minutes.

Wendy Lee Paffenroth, *Pine Island, NY*

Nutty French Toast Bake

A great breakfast is in store when this is paired up with a side of fluffy scrambled eggs.

Serves 6 to 8

1 loaf French bread, torn into bite-size pieces
1 t. cinnamon
1 c. chopped nuts
1/2 c. raisins
6 eggs, beaten
1 t. vanilla extract
1 c. half-and-half
1 c. milk
1/2 c. maple syrup
1/2 c. brown sugar, packed
1/2 c. butter, melted

Mix bread, cinnamon, nuts and raisins together; spoon into a greased 13"x9" baking pan. Set aside. Beat eggs, vanilla, half-and-half and milk together; stir in maple syrup. Pour over bread; sprinkle with brown sugar. Drizzle with butter; refrigerate for at least one hour. Bake at 350 degrees for 45 minutes to one hour.

Athena Colegrove, *Big Springs, TX*

Sweetie Banana Oatmeal

My little ones, with Daddy's help, made this for me on Valentine's Day...what a yummy breakfast surprise from my 3 sweeties!

Serves 4

2 c. long-cooking oats, uncooked
1/2 c. sweetened condensed milk
4 c. water
2 bananas, thinly sliced

Combine oats, milk and water in a slow cooker that has been sprayed with non-stick vegetable spray. Cover and cook on low setting for 6 to 8 hours. Add bananas 10 to 15 minutes before serving.

Sweetie Banana Oatmeal

Blueberry & Cream Cheese Strata

Marybeth Biggins, *Brockton, MA*

French Toast Soufflé

I prepare this recipe for a "girls only" brunch that my friends and I take turns hosting once a month. It is so good!

Serves 6 to 8

10 c. bread, cubed
8-oz. pkg. cream cheese, softened
8 eggs, beaten
1-1/2 c. milk
2/3 c. half-and-half
1/2 c. maple syrup
1/2 t. vanilla extract
3/4 t. cinnamon
2 T. powdered sugar

Place bread in a greased 13"x9" baking pan; set aside. Beat cream cheese until smooth; add eggs. Mix well; stir in milk, half-and-half, maple syrup, vanilla and cinnamon. Blend until smooth; pour over bread. Bake at 375 degrees for 50 minutes; sprinkle with powdered sugar.

Kathy Grashoff, *Fort Wayne, IN*

Blueberry & Cream Cheese Strata

This berry-filled strata is just right for a leisurely breakfast with family & friends.

Serves 4 to 6

16-oz. loaf white bread, crusts removed, cubed and divided
2 c. frozen blueberries, divided
3-oz. pkg. cream cheese, cut into 1/4-inch cubes
4 eggs, beaten
2 c. milk
1/3 c. sugar
1 t. vanilla extract
1/4 t. salt
1/4 t. nutmeg

Place half of the bread in a greased 8"x8" baking pan; top with half of the blueberries. Top with cream cheese, remaining bread and remaining blueberries; set aside. Beat eggs, milk, sugar, vanilla, salt and nutmeg with an electric mixer on medium speed until blended. Pour over bread mixture and refrigerate for 20 minutes to overnight. Bake, uncovered, at 325 degrees for one hour.

Anne Muns, *Scottsdale, AZ*

Garden-Fresh Egg Casserole

Fresh tomatoes and spinach turn this breakfast casserole into something extra special. I think it's perfect for overnight guests.

Serves 8 to 10

1 c. buttermilk
1/2 c. onion, grated
1-1/2 c. shredded Monterey Jack cheese
1 c. cottage cheese
1 c. spinach, chopped
1 c. tomatoes, chopped
1/2 c. butter, melted
1-1/2 doz. eggs, beaten

Mix all ingredients together; pour into a greased 13"x9" baking pan. Cover; refrigerate overnight. Bake at 350 degrees for 50 minutes to one hour.

Jane White, *Kountze, TX*

Morning Delight

So delicious and easy to make...no one can resist it!

Serves 6 to 8

2 8-oz. tubes refrigerated crescent rolls, divided
2 8-oz. pkgs. cream cheese, softened
1 egg, beaten
1 T. almond extract
1 c. sugar
Garnish: sugar, cinnamon to taste
Optional: sliced bananas

Press one tube of crescent rolls into the bottom of a greased 13"x9" baking pan; seal seams. Set aside. Mix cream cheese, egg, extract and sugar in a bowl; spread over rolls in pan. Top with remaining crescent rolls; sprinkle to taste with sugar and cinnamon. Bake at 350 degrees for 20 to 25 minutes, until golden. Top with sliced bananas, if desired.

Flavor Booster

······· ✳ ·······

A fresh breakfast side dish...fruit kabobs! Just slide pineapple chunks, apple slices, grapes, orange wedges and strawberries onto a wooden skewer. They can even be slipped into breakfast smoothies or frosty juices.

Morning Delight

Cheese, Bacon & Potato Tart

Kathy Grashoff, *Fort Wayne, IN*

Cheesy Chicken Brunch Bake

Ideal for a Mothers' Day brunch or anytime you're getting together with friends. Have plenty of fresh fruit to go alongside servings.

Serves 6 to 8

3 c. chicken broth
10-3/4 oz. can cream of chicken soup
9 slices bread, cubed
4 c. cooked chicken, cubed
1/2 c. instant rice, uncooked
1 c. shredded sharp Cheddar cheese, divided
2 T. fresh parsley, minced
1-1/2 t. salt
4 eggs, beaten

Combine broth with soup in a large bowl. Add bread and toss to coat. Add chicken, rice, 3/4 cup cheese, parsley and salt; mix well. Pour into a greased 13"x9" baking pan. Pour eggs over all and sprinkle with remaining cheese. Bake, uncovered, at 325 degrees for one hour.

Kristi Vandenham, *Fillmore, CA*

Cheese, Bacon & Potato Tart

This is delicious with whatever cheese you have on hand.

Serves 8

1 T. butter
1 lb. bacon
1-1/2 lbs. potatoes, peeled, sliced and divided
1-1/4 c. shredded Cheddar cheese, divided
salt and pepper to taste

Spread butter in an 8" round baking pan; place bacon over butter, arranging in spoke-like fashion. Bring bacon up the sides and over the edge of the pan. Top with half the potatoes; sprinkle with half the cheese. Layer with remaining potatoes and cheese; top with salt and pepper. Fold ends of bacon slices across the top; bake at 400 degrees for about one hour, or until potatoes are tender.

~ *Cook it Quick* ~

Are family members on different schedules? Divide the ingredients for a breakfast casserole among individual ramekins and bake as needed.

Lynda Purvis, *Anchorage, AK*

Apple-Cinnamon French Toast

Yummy topped with warm maple, apricot, blueberry or raspberry syrup.

Serves 4 to 6

4 slices French bread, crusts removed, cubed
   and divided
8-oz. pkg. cream cheese, cubed
1 apple, peeled, cored and chopped
6 eggs, beaten
1 c. milk
1-1/2 t. cinnamon
2 to 3 T. powdered sugar

Place half of the bread into an ungreased 11"x7" baking pan. Top with cream cheese. Sprinkle with apple; top with remaining bread. Set aside. Beat eggs, milk and cinnamon together; pour over bread mixture. Bake at 375 degrees for 35 minutes, or until set; sprinkle with powdered sugar.

Darcie Stearns, *Rock Island, IL*

Pecan French Toast

This overnight, oven-baked French toast will win you raves!

Serves 6 to 8

1 loaf French bread, sliced
6 eggs, beaten
1-1/2 c. milk
1-1/2 c. half-and-half
1 t. vanilla extract
1/8 t. nutmeg
1 t. cinnamon

Arrange bread in a lightly greased 13"x9" baking pan; set aside. Beat together remaining ingredients; pour over bread. Cover; refrigerate overnight. Spread Topping over mixture; bake at 350 degrees for 45 to 55 minutes. Let stand 5 minutes before serving.

Topping:
1/2 c. butter, softened
2 T. maple syrup
1 c. brown sugar, packed
1 c. chopped pecans

Mix all ingredients together.

Pecan French Toast

Southern Corned Beef Hash

Tracie Daugherty, *Kittanning, PA*

Tracie's Ham & Spinach Quiche

My family enjoys this easy dish morning, noon or night. Try adding a different cheese or veggie for a change.

Serves 6 to 8

1 doz. eggs, beaten
1 pt. whipping cream
1/2 t. garlic powder
1/2 t. dried oregano
1/8 t. pepper
1 c. cooked ham, finely diced
10-oz. pkg. frozen spinach, cooked and drained
1/3 c. onion, finely diced
8-oz. pkg. shredded Cheddar cheese

Beat together eggs and cream, blending well. Add seasonings; mix well. Sprinkle ham, spinach, onion and cheese evenly into a lightly greased 13"x9" baking pan; slowly pour egg mixture over top. Bake at 350 degrees for 45 to 50 minutes, until top is golden and knife inserted into center comes out clean. Cool slightly before cutting into squares.

Tammy Williams, *West Carthage, NY*

Southern Corned Beef Hash

Top each portion with an egg cooked sunny-side up.

Serves 4 to 6

1 to 2 T. oil
6 to 8 potatoes, peeled, diced and cooked
1 onion, diced
2 12-oz. cans corned beef, diced
salt and pepper to taste

Heat oil in a large skillet over medium heat; add potatoes, onion and corned beef. Cook over low heat for about 10 minutes, until crisp and golden. Add salt and pepper to taste.

Becky Woods, *Ballwin, MO*

Smoked Gouda Grits

Serve with scrambled eggs and breakfast sausage!

Serves 6 to 8

6 c. chicken broth
2 c. milk
1 t. salt
1/2 t. white pepper
2 c. quick-cooking grits, uncooked
1-2/3 c. smoked Gouda cheese, shredded
3 T. butter, softened

Bring broth, milk, salt and pepper to a boil in a large saucepan over medium heat. Gradually whisk in grits. Reduce heat; cover and simmer, stirring occasionally, for about 5 minutes, until thickened. Add cheese and butter; stir until melted.

∼ Cook it Quick ∼

A fun centerpiece for the breakfast table! Thread doughnut holes on long wooden skewers and arrange in a vase for easy serving. Yum!

Liz Plotnick-Snay, *Gooseberry Patch*

Autumn Apple-Walnut Pancake

Oven-baked and filled with the best flavors of fall.

Serves 4

3 T. butter, divided
2 apples, peeled, cored and thinly sliced
1/3 c. brown sugar, packed
1/2 t. cinnamon
1/8 t. nutmeg
1/2 c. chopped walnuts, toasted
4 eggs, beaten
1 c. milk
1 c. all-purpose flour
1 t. baking powder
Garnish: powdered sugar, maple syrup

Melt 2 tablespoons butter over medium heat in a large oven-proof skillet. Add apples, sugar and spices; cook and stir until apples are soft and just golden, about 7 minutes. Add walnuts; cook and stir until apples are caramelized, 2 to 3 minutes. Add remaining butter; stir to melt. Remove from heat. In a large bowl, combine eggs, milk, flour and baking powder; whisk just until blended. Pour batter over apple mixture in skillet. Bake at 400 degrees for 15 to 20 minutes, until puffy and golden. Cut into wedges; sprinkle with sugar or drizzle with syrup, as desired. Serve immediately.

Autumn Apple-Walnut Pancake

Garden Quiche

Marsha Konken, Sterling, CO

Potato-Bacon Breakfast Pie

Just add cinnamon rolls and fresh fruit for a complete meal.

Serves 4 to 6

1 lb. bacon, crisply cooked and crumbled
9-inch pie crust
2 c. frozen shredded hashbrowns, thawed
1/2 c. shredded Cheddar cheese
4 eggs, beaten
1/4 c. milk

Arrange bacon in pie crust; layer evenly with hashbrowns and cheese. Combine eggs and milk; pour over cheese. Bake at 350 degrees for 40 minutes, or until center is set. Let stand for 5 minutes before slicing into wedges.

Sharon Tillman, Hampton, VA

Garden Quiche

This yummy stovetop quiche is a clever way to use up odds & ends of fresh veggies and cheese from the fridge...feel free to substitute what you have on hand! Sometimes we enjoy it with a cup of tomato soup as a pleasant light lunch.

Makes 2 to 4 servings

1 T. butter
1/4 c. onion, finely chopped
2 T. green or red pepper, chopped
1 clove garlic, minced
1/2 lb. yellow squash, thinly sliced
1/2 lb. broccoli flowerets, coarsely chopped
2 eggs, beaten
1/4 c. milk
1/8 t. cayenne pepper
1/4 t. dry mustard
1/4 t. dried marjoram
1/2 c. shredded Swiss cheese
2 T. grated Parmesan cheese

Melt butter in a skillet over medium heat. Add onion and green or red pepper; sauté until soft and golden. Stir in garlic, squash and broccoli; cover and cook for 3 to 5 minutes, just until tender. Whisk together eggs, milk and seasonings; stir in Swiss cheese. Pour mixture over vegetables in skillet; sprinkle with Parmesan cheese. Reduce heat to low. Cover and cook for 5 minutes, or just until eggs are set and cheese has melted. Cut into wedges.

Traci Green, *Orange Park, FL*

Hashbrown Breakfast Pizza

Let the kids help put together this fun breakfast dish... they'll love eating their creation.

Serves 6

8-oz. tube refrigerated crescent rolls
1 lb. ground pork sausage, browned and drained
1 c. shredded Cheddar cheese
2 T. grated Parmesan cheese
1 c. frozen shredded hashbrowns, thawed
5 eggs, beaten
1/4 c. milk
1/2 t. salt
1/8 t. pepper

Separate rolls and press together to form a crust on an ungreased 12" pizza pan. Layer with sausage, cheeses and hashbrowns; set aside. Whisk eggs, milk, salt and pepper together and pour over hashbrowns. Bake at 375 degrees for 30 minutes. Cut into wedges.

Laura Fuller, *Fort Wayne, IN*

Creamed Eggs

Spoon over buttered toast...real comfort food.

Makes 3 servings

1/4 c. butter
1/4 c. all-purpose flour
2 c. milk
6 eggs, hard-boiled, peeled and diced
salt and pepper to taste

Melt butter in a large saucepan over medium heat; stir in flour. Slowly add milk; continue stirring over medium heat. When desired thickness is reached, fold in eggs and heat through. Add salt and pepper to taste.

～ Cook it Quick ～

Breakfast foods are so warm and comforting...try 'em for dinner as a special treat! Scrambled eggs and toast or pancakes and bacon are easy to stir up in minutes. Or assemble a family-favorite breakfast casserole in the morning and pop it in the oven at dinnertime.

Hashbrown Breakfast Pizza

Potato & Onion Frittata

Wendy Jacobs, Idaho Falls, ID

Potato & Onion Frittata

Make a hearty, warm breakfast using a little leftover ham and potato from last night's dinner.

Makes 4 servings

2 to 3 T. olive oil, divided
1 yellow onion, peeled and thinly sliced
1/4 c. cooked ham, diced
1 c. potatoes, peeled, cooked and diced
4 eggs, beaten
1/3 c. shredded Parmesan cheese
salt to taste

Heat 2 tablespoons oil over medium heat in a non-stick skillet. Add onion; cook and stir for 2 to 3 minutes. Add ham and potatoes. Cook until onion and potatoes are lightly golden. With a slotted spoon, remove mixture to a bowl; cool slightly. Stir eggs, cheese and salt into onion mixture. Return skillet to medium heat; add the remaining oil, if needed. When skillet is hot, add onion mixture. Cook until frittata is golden on the bottom and top begins to set, about 4 to 5 minutes. Place a plate over skillet and carefully invert frittata onto the plate. Slide frittata back into skillet. Cook until bottom is lightly golden, 2 to 3 minutes. Cut into wedges; serve warm or at room temperature.

Janice Miller, Huntington, IN

Overnight Pumpkin French Toast

Brioche bread is my favorite for this recipe. You can bake this right away, but it's best if refrigerated overnight.

Serves 6

15-oz. can pumpkin
6 eggs, beaten
3 egg yolks, beaten
4 c. milk
1 c. whipping cream
1-1/2 c. sugar
1 t. vanilla extract
1 loaf bread, sliced 1-1/2 inches thick
Garnish: maple syrup, whipped cream, chopped nuts

Mix together all ingredients except bread and garnish. Arrange bread in a lightly greased 13"x9" baking pan; pour pumpkin mixture over top. Cover and refrigerate overnight. Bake at 425 degrees for about 30 minutes. Top with maple syrup, whipped cream and chopped nuts.

Chapter Two

Hearty Soups & Stews

Warm and filling, soups and stews are perfect for quick lunches and easy dinners. From chowders to chilis and everything in between, you'll find our best recipes to warm you to your toes. Beefy Nacho Cheese Soup is oh-so delicious, and has only 5 ingredients. Chicken Stew Over Biscuits will have your family begging for second helpings. Smoky Sausage Stew goes together in a jiffy, and Speedy Chicken Gumbo will become a staple at your house!

Marlene Darnell, *Newport Beach, CA*

Smoky Sausage Stew

Add a little hot pepper sauce, if you like.

Serves 6

14-1/2 oz. can beef broth, divided
14-1/2 oz. can stewed tomatoes
16-oz. pkg. smoked bratwurst, sliced
4 new potatoes, cubed
2 onions, coarsely chopped
1 c. baby carrots
1/4 c. all-purpose flour
1 green pepper, diced

Set aside 1/4 cup beef broth. Combine remaining beef broth, tomatoes with juice, bratwurst, potatoes, onions and carrots in a large stockpot over medium heat. Bring to a boil; reduce heat and simmer for 15 to 20 minutes, until vegetables are tender. Combine reserved broth with flour, stirring until smooth; stir into pot until thickened. Add green pepper; simmer 3 minutes.

Kathy Harris, *Valley Center, KS*

Speedy Chicken Gumbo

This gumbo is a staple at our house because it can be made quickly and transported easily. It's delicious served over cornbread.

Serves 6

3 T. oil
1/3 c. all-purpose flour
1 onion, chopped
2 red peppers, chopped
3 cloves garlic, minced
1 t. dried oregano
salt and pepper to taste
4 c. water
10-oz. pkg. frozen cut okra, thawed
8-oz. smoked andouille sausage, halved lengthwise and sliced 1-inch thick
1 deli roast chicken, boned and shredded

In a large stockpot, heat oil over medium heat. Add flour; cook for 5 to 7 minutes, whisking constantly, until golden. Stir in onion, red peppers, garlic and oregano. Season with salt and pepper. Cook, stirring constantly, until vegetables are crisp-tender, about 10 to 12 minutes. Add water; stir in okra and sausage. Bring to a boil. Stir in shredded chicken and warm through.

Speedy Chicken Gumbo

New England Fish Chowder

Lynda Robson, *Boston, MA*

New England Fish Chowder

Such a hearty and flavorful chowder. Garnish with oyster crackers and chopped green onion for a perfect treat.

Makes 6 servings

1 T. oil
1/2 c. onion, chopped
2-1/2 c. potatoes, peeled and diced
1-1/2 c. boiling water
salt and pepper to taste
1 lb. frozen cod or haddock fillets, thawed and cut into
    large chunks
2 c. milk
1 T. butter

Heat oil in a large saucepan over medium heat. Add onion and sauté until tender. Add potatoes, water, salt and pepper. Reduce heat; cover and simmer for 15 to 20 minutes, until potatoes are tender. Add fish; simmer until fish flakes easily with a fork, about 5 minutes. Just before serving, add milk and butter; stir well and heat through.

Handy Tip

⁕

A loaf of sourdough bread is a tasty partner for a hearty pot of chowder...pick up a ready-made loaf at the market and pop it in the oven for a crisp, warm crust!

Mary Jo Babiarz, *Spring Grove, IL*

Chilly Weather Chili

Garnish with Cheddar cheese stars that have been cut out with cookie cutters.

Serves 4

1 lb. ground beef
2 T. onion, diced
15-3/4 oz. can chili beans with chili sauce
8-1/4 oz. can refried beans
8-oz. can tomato sauce
8-oz. jar salsa
1/2 c. water

Brown beef and onion together in a large stockpot; drain. Add remaining ingredients. Bring to a boil and reduce heat to medium; cover and simmer for 30 minutes, stirring occasionally.

Amy Woods, *Gainesville, TX*

Cabbage Patch Stew

A creamy, cheesy cabbage stew with a little chile kick! Substitute plain diced tomatoes if your family prefers milder dishes.

Serves 6 to 8

2 lbs. ground beef
1 head cabbage, chopped
2 10-3/4 oz. cans cream of mushroom soup
2 10-3/4 oz. cans Cheddar cheese soup
2 10-oz. cans diced tomatoes with green chiles

Place ground beef in a large stockpot; sauté until browned. Drain. Add cabbage and just enough water to cover. Simmer until cabbage is tender; add remaining ingredients. Simmer for 20 minutes.

Gretchen Ham, *Pine City, NY*

Sunday Meeting Tomato Soup

Fresh basil really makes this soup special. It's often requested at our church's Sunday soup & sandwich lunches after the services.

Makes 10 servings

1/2 c. butter, sliced
1 c. fresh basil, chopped
2 28-oz. cans crushed tomatoes
2 cloves garlic, minced
1 qt. half-and-half
salt and pepper to taste
Garnish: croutons, shredded Parmesan cheese

In a large saucepan, melt butter over medium heat. Add basil; sauté for 2 minutes. Add tomatoes with juice and garlic. Reduce heat and simmer for 20 minutes. Remove from heat; let cool slightly. Working in batches, transfer tomato mixture to a blender and purée. Transfer back into saucepan and add half-and-half, mixing well. Reheat soup over medium-low heat; add salt and pepper to taste. Serve topped with croutons and shredded Parmesan cheese.

~ *Simple Swap* ~
Easily substitute ground chicken, turkey or pork for ground beef in most soups and stews.

Sunday Meeting Tomato Soup

Chicken & Apple Wild Rice Soup

Tyson Ann Trecannelli, *Gettysburg, PA*

Chicken & Apple Wild Rice Soup

This is a simple, hearty and delicious soup...so fragrant and sure to call everyone to the table. A perfect dish for fall get-togethers when apples are plentiful.

Serves 8 to 10

2 T. olive oil
2 carrots, peeled and chopped
1 onion, chopped
3 stalks celery, chopped
4 qts. chicken broth
4 boneless, skinless chicken breasts, cooked and
    shredded
1/3 c. wild rice, uncooked
2 t. dried tarragon
1 T. fresh parsley, chopped
salt and pepper to taste
3 Granny Smith apples, peeled, cored and chopped

Heat oil in a stockpot over medium heat. Sauté vegetables until tender, about 10 minutes. Add remaining ingredients except apples. Reduce heat to medium-low; cover and simmer for 45 minutes. Add apples and simmer for an additional 40 minutes, or until apples are tender and rice is cooked.

Kimberly Basore, *Garland, TX*

Easy Goulash

Replace the kidney beans with navy beans, if you prefer.

Serves 4 to 6

1 lb. ground beef
1/4 c. onion, chopped
14-1/2 oz. can stewed tomatoes
3/4 c. water
salt and pepper to taste
2 c. elbow macaroni, uncooked
15-1/4 oz. can corn, drained
15-oz. can kidney beans, drained and rinsed
16-oz. pkg. pasteurized process cheese spread, cubed

Brown beef and onion in a large stockpot over medium heat; drain. Add tomatoes with juice and water; sprinkle with salt and pepper to taste. Add macaroni and simmer for 8 to 10 minutes, until macaroni is tender, adding more water if necessary. Add corn, beans and cheese; heat until cheese is melted.

Carrie Knotts, *Kalispell, MT*

Lentil-Barley Vegetable Stew

When my grandmother "MaMaw Lou" passed away, all I wanted were her cookbooks. I found this recipe in one of them and just love it.

Serves 4

4 carrots, peeled and diced
2 leeks, diced
2 stalks celery, diced
2 zucchini, diced
1 onion, chopped
1/2 c. okra, sliced
1 c. dried lentils, uncooked
1/2 c. pearled barley, uncooked
6 to 7 c. vegetable broth
1 c. fresh basil, torn
1/4 c. olive oil
1 T. garlic, minced
1 t. dried thyme

Combine all ingredients in a large pot. Bring to a boil; reduce heat to medium. Simmer until lentils and barley are tender, about 30 minutes.

Amy Butcher, *Columbus, GA*

Dijon Beef Stew

A loaf of crusty French bread, a salad of mixed greens and steaming bowls of this stew...aah. What could be any better?

Serves 6 to 8

1-1/2 lbs. stew beef cubes
1/4 c. all-purpose flour
2 T. oil
salt and pepper to taste
2 14-1/2 oz. cans diced tomatoes with garlic and onion
14-1/2 oz. can beef broth
4 carrots, peeled and cut into bite-size pieces
2 potatoes, peeled and cut into bite-size pieces
3/4 t. dried thyme
2 T. Dijon mustard

Combine beef and flour in a large plastic zipping bag; toss to coat evenly. Add oil to a stockpot over medium-high heat. Brown beef; sprinkle with salt and pepper. Add tomatoes with juice and remaining ingredients except mustard. Bring to a boil; reduce heat. Cover and simmer for one hour, or until beef is tender. Stir in mustard.

Dijon Beef Stew

Chicken Noodle Gumbo

Lorrie Smith, Drummonds, TN

Chicken Noodle Gumbo

This colorful dish makes enough to feed a whole bunch of hungry folks! Look for the "gumbo blend" of frozen vegetables at the market.

Serves 8 to 10

2 lbs. boneless, skinless chicken breasts, cut into
   1-inch cubes
4 16-oz. cans chicken broth
15-oz. can diced tomatoes
32-oz. pkg. frozen okra, corn, celery and red pepper
   mixed vegetables
8-oz. pkg. bowtie pasta, uncooked
1/2 t. garlic powder
salt and pepper to taste

Place chicken, broth and tomatoes in a large soup pot. Bring to a boil over medium heat. Reduce heat; simmer 10 minutes. Add frozen vegetables, uncooked pasta and seasonings. Return to a boil; reduce heat to medium-low. Cover and simmer one hour.

∼ Handy Tip ∼

A nice thermos full of delicious hot soup and fresh baked rolls wrapped up in a neat towel make a tummy-warming present for a friend or neighbor.

Lynn Williams, Muncie, IN

Hearty Turkey-Veggie Soup

Chock-full of vegetables and turkey...a soup to be thankful for!

Serves 6

1 T. olive oil
2 t. garlic, minced
28-oz. can diced tomatoes
8-oz. pkg. sliced mushrooms
12-oz. jar pearl onions, drained
2 c. water
1-1/2 lbs. potatoes, peeled and diced
2 carrots, peeled and diced
2 stalks celery, sliced
1 t. dried thyme
1/2 t. dried rosemary
2 bay leaves
1/2 t. salt
2-1/2 lbs. skinless turkey thighs
10-oz. pkg. frozen peas, thawed
1-1/2 c. frozen corn, thawed
1/2 c. fresh parsley, minced
pepper to taste

Heat oil in a Dutch oven over medium heat; add garlic and sauté for 10 seconds. Add tomatoes and mushrooms with juice, onions, water, potatoes, carrots, celery, herbs and salt. Arrange turkey thighs over vegetables. Bring to a boil over high heat; reduce heat to medium-low. Cover and simmer, stirring occasionally, for about one hour, until turkey juices run clear. Remove turkey to a plate; discard bones and cut into bite-size pieces. Return turkey to pan. Stir in peas, corn and parsley; simmer until heated through, about 3 to 5 minutes. Add pepper to taste. Discard bay leaves before serving.

Kimberly Hancock, *Murrieta, CA*

Country Chicken Chowder

This chowder is a snap to make and oh-so hearty...it's a meal in a bowl! Garnish individual servings with a dollop of sour cream and a sprinkle of dill weed.

Serves 8

2 T. butter
1-1/2 lbs. chicken tenders, sliced into 1/2-inch pieces
2 10-3/4 oz. cans cream of potato soup
1-1/2 c. chicken broth
2 onions, chopped
2 stalks celery, sliced
2 carrots, peeled and sliced
2 c. frozen corn
1 t. dill weed
1/2 c. half-and-half

Melt butter in a skillet over medium heat. Add chicken and cook until golden. Place chicken in a slow cooker; stir in remaining ingredients except half-and-half. Cover and cook on low setting for 3 to 4 hours. Shortly before serving time, turn off slow cooker; stir in half-and-half. Cover and let stand for 5 to 10 minutes, just until heated through.

Sharon Laney, *Mogadore, OH*

Green Pepper Soup

Fall brings thoughts of a bountiful harvest with gardens and roadside stands overflowing with fresh vegetables...and this hearty soup.

Makes 8 to 10 servings

2 lbs. ground beef
28-oz. can tomato sauce
28-oz. can diced tomatoes
2 c. cooked rice
2 c. green peppers, chopped
2 cubes beef bouillon
1/4 c. brown sugar, packed
2 t. pepper

In a stockpot over medium heat, brown beef; drain. Add remaining ingredients and bring to a boil. Reduce heat; cover and simmer for 30 to 40 minutes, until peppers are tender.

Green Pepper Soup

Kielbasa Soup

Pamela Bennett, *Whittier, CA*

Kielbasa Soup

My mom made up this recipe one evening when there wasn't a lot to eat in the house. It has since become a favorite comfort food!

Makes 8 to 10 servings

1 head cabbage, shredded
16-oz. pkg. Kielbasa sausage, sliced
2 16-oz. cans diced tomatoes
1 onion, chopped
2 zucchini, quartered and sliced
2 yellow squash, quartered and sliced
2 T. seasoned salt
2 cloves garlic, crushed
1 cube beef bouillon
1 t. dried oregano
2 redskin or russet potatoes, cubed

In a stockpot, combine all ingredients except potatoes. Cover ingredients with water; bring to a boil. Cover, reduce heat and simmer for 1-1/2 to 2 hours. Add potatoes during last 30 minutes of cook time.

Sharon Tillman, *Hampton, VA*

Shipwreck Stew

My boys were always such picky eaters...unless there was Shipwreck Stew for dinner! The recipe's unusual name really fascinated them, and they would eat every bite.

Serves 6

1 lb. ground beef, browned and drained
2 16-oz. cans kidney beans
10-3/4 oz. can tomato soup
5 potatoes, peeled and cubed
1/2 green pepper, diced
1/2 onion, diced
1/4 c. long-cooking rice, uncooked
1 t. Worcestershire sauce
1 t. chili powder
1 c. water

Combine all ingredients in a slow cooker; mix well. Cover and cook on high setting for 4 to 6 hours.

Handy Tip

A simple trick to skim the fat from a pot of soup! When you start your soup, place a metal spoon in the freezer. When soup is done, use the chilled spoon to skim the surface. The fat will stick to the spoon.

Leath Sarvo, *Cincinnati, OH*

Vegetarian Cincinnati Chili

A meatless version of a local tradition! Serve over cooked spaghetti for 2-way chili or topped with shredded cheese for 3-way chili.

Serves 6

46-oz. can tomato juice
16-oz. can kidney beans, drained and rinsed
1 onion, chopped
2 T. chili powder
1-1/2 t. white vinegar
1 t. allspice
1 t. cinnamon
1 t. pepper
1 t. ground cumin
1/8 t. garlic powder
1/4 t. Worcestershire sauce
5 bay leaves

Combine all ingredients in a slow cooker. Cover and cook on low setting for 5 hours. Discard bay leaves before serving.

Denise Webb, *Galveston, IN*

Meatball-Vegetable Cheese Soup

You'll want to try this slow-cooker recipe...it's a real family-pleaser!

Serves 6

1 lb. ground beef
1/4 c. dry bread crumbs
1 egg, beaten
1/2 t. salt
1/2 t. hot pepper sauce
1 c. celery, chopped
1/2 c. onion, chopped
2 cubes beef bouillon
1 c. corn
1 c. potato, peeled and diced
1/2 c. carrot, peeled and sliced
2 c. water
16-oz. jar pasteurized process cheese sauce

In a bowl, mix together beef, bread crumbs, egg, salt and hot sauce; form into one-inch balls. Place in a slow cooker. Add remaining ingredients except cheese sauce. Cover and cook on low setting for 8 to 10 hours. Immediately before serving, stir in cheese sauce until combined. Cover and cook an additional 10 minutes, or until warmed through.

Meatball-Vegetable Cheese Soup

Pepper Jack-Crab Bisque

Wendy Ball, Battle Creek, MI

Pepper Jack-Crab Bisque

My husband and I enjoyed a soup like this when dining out with our good friends, Rick and Carolyn. My efforts to recreate it really paid off...we love it!

Makes 6 servings

2 T. butter
2 stalks celery, finely chopped
1 onion, finely chopped
2 10-3/4 oz. cans tomato bisque or tomato soup
2-1/2 c. whipping cream or half-and-half
3 8-oz. pkgs. imitation crabmeat, flaked
1-1/2 c. shredded Pepper Jack cheese

Melt butter in a stockpot over medium heat. Add celery and onion; cook until softened. Add bisque or soup, cream or half-and-half and crabmeat. Simmer over low heat until heated through; stir in cheese. If too thick, add a little more cream or half-and-half as desired.

Susie Backus, Delaware, OH

Chicken & Broccoli Chowder

Warms you right down to your toes!

Makes 4 to 6 servings

1 lb. boneless, skinless chicken thighs, cubed
14-1/2 oz. can chicken broth
1/2 c. water
1 c. baby carrots, sliced
1 c. sliced mushrooms
1/2 c. onion, chopped
1/4 t. garlic powder
1/8 t. dried thyme
10-3/4 oz. can cream of chicken & broccoli soup
1/2 c. milk
3 T. all-purpose flour
10-oz. pkg. frozen broccoli, thawed

Combine chicken, broth, water, carrots, mushrooms, onion and seasonings in a slow cooker; mix well. Cover and cook on low setting for 7 to 9 hours. In a small bowl, whisk together soup, milk and flour; stir into slow cooker along with broccoli. Cover and cook an additional 30 minutes, or until broccoli is tender.

Patty Habig Bowen, *Westfield, NY*

Creamy Chicken & Wild Rice Soup

I've tweaked this slow-cooker recipe so many times, it's nothing like the original! It's so thick, you can use the leftovers for chicken pot pie filling.

Serves 8 to 10

4 boneless, skinless chicken breasts, cubed
3/4 lb. carrots, peeled and sliced
3 stalks celery, sliced
1 onion, diced
2 4.3-oz. pkgs. long-grain and wild rice mix
4 10-3/4 oz. cans cream of potato soup
32-oz. container chicken broth
2 c. whipping cream

In a slow cooker, layer chicken, carrot, celery, onion, rice with seasoning packets and potato soup. Pour broth over top. Cover and cook on low setting for 8 hours. Stir thoroughly. Mix in cream; cover and heat through, about 15 minutes.

Darci Heaton, *Woodbury, PA*

Egg Drop Soup

My daughter and I love egg drop soup, so we played around with different ingredients until we came up with this recipe. We love it more than our local Chinese restaurant's version!

Serves 4 to 6

8 c. chicken broth, divided
1 cube chicken bouillon
3 T. cornstarch
4 eggs, well beaten
Optional: wide chow mein noodles

Add 6-1/2 cups broth and bouillon cube to a soup pot over medium-high heat; bring to a boil. In a bowl, add cornstarch to remaining broth; stir until dissolved. Pour cornstarch mixture into boiling broth and stir. Bring broth to a rolling boil. With a fork, drizzle eggs into boiling broth; eggs should cook immediately. Simmer for one to 2 minutes. Serve topped with chow mein noodles, if desired.

Creamy Chicken & Wild Rice Soup

Fred's Chunky Chili

Marian Muder, *Hubbard, OH*

Fred's Chunky Chili

My husband has been making his signature chili for years now. It's a combination of several tasty recipes.

Serves 4 to 6

1 lb. ground beef or turkey, browned and drained
3/4 c. green pepper, diced
1 t. garlic, minced
3/4 c. onion, diced
6-oz. can tomato paste
14-1/2 oz. can stewed tomatoes
15-1/2 oz. can kidney beans
1/4 c. salsa
1 T. sugar
1/2 t. cayenne pepper
1/2 t. dried cilantro
1 t. dried basil
Garnish: shredded Cheddar cheese, crackers

Combine all ingredients except garnish in a Dutch oven. Bring to a simmer over medium-high heat. Cover and simmer over low heat for 30 minutes, stirring occasionally and adding a little water, if needed. Serve with cheese and crackers.

Jennifer Oglesby, *Brownsville, IN*

Homestyle Chicken Stew

This is so good on a chilly autumn or winter day, along with homemade bread...mmm!

Serves 4

1 lb. boneless, skinless chicken breasts, cubed
2 c. potatoes, peeled and cubed
1 stalk celery, sliced
2 carrots, peeled and sliced
14-1/2 oz. can chicken broth
6-oz. can tomato paste
1/2 t. celery seed
1/2 t. paprika
1/4 t. pepper
1/4 t. dried thyme
1-1/2 T. cold water
1 T. cornstarch

In a slow cooker, combine all ingredients except water and cornstarch. Mix together well. Cover and cook on low setting for 7 to 8 hours, or on high setting for 3-1/2 hours. About 30 minutes before serving time, stir water and cornstarch together and stir into stew. Cook, covered, for an additional 30 minutes, or until thickened.

Cook it Quick

A Soup Supper menu shouldn't be fussy and the serving style is "help yourself!" A variety of soups, along with some biscuits and rolls and a crock of creamery butter is all that's needed. No kitchen duty at this gathering... the idea is to relax and enjoy the season together.

Penny McShane, *Lombard, IL*

Split Pea Soup

Choose either green or yellow split peas as you like.

Makes 4 to 6 servings

16-oz. pkg. dried split peas
1 c. onion, chopped
1/2 c. celery, chopped
1/2 c. carrots, peeled and sliced
3 cubes chicken bouillon
1 bay leaf
1 t. salt
1/4 t. pepper
1-1/2 c. cooked ham, diced

Soak peas in water overnight; drain and rinse. Combine peas and remaining ingredients except ham in a slow cooker; cover with water. Cover and cook on low setting for 8 to 10 hours, until soup is thick. Add ham during the last hour; discard bay leaf before serving.

Angie O'Keefe, *Soddy Daisy, TN*

Pioneer Beef Stew

There's nothing more satisfying than a hearty bowl of beef stew! It's baked, not simmered on the stovetop... no need to watch it.

Serves 4 to 6

14-1/2 oz. can petite diced tomatoes
1 c. water
3 T. quick-cooking tapioca, uncooked
2 t. sugar
1-1/2 t. salt
1/2 t. pepper
1-1/2 lbs. stew beef cubes
3 to 4 potatoes, peeled and cubed
4 carrots, peeled and thickly sliced
1 onion, diced

In a large bowl, combine tomatoes with juice, water, tapioca, sugar, salt and pepper. Mix well; stir in remaining ingredients. Pour into a greased 3-quart casserole dish. Cover and bake at 375 degrees for 1-1/2 to 2 hours, until beef and vegetables are tender.

Pioneer Beef Stew

Macaroni & Cheese Chowder

Alissa Sellers, *Bangor, PA*

Macaroni & Cheese Chowder

This recipe is a family favorite that even my young son loves! It's perfect for a quick family dinner, especially on a cold or rainy night.

Serves 4 to 6

14-oz. can chicken broth
1 c. water
1 c. elbow macaroni, uncooked
1 c. milk
8-oz. pkg. pasteurized process cheese spread
1 c. cooked ham, diced
1 c. corn

Over medium heat, bring broth and water to a boil in a saucepan. Add macaroni and cook until tender, about 12 minutes. Reduce heat to low. Add milk, cheese, ham and corn. Simmer and stir until cheese is melted.

Flavor Booster

························ ✳ ························

A sprinkle of herbs can really perk up the flavor of soup. Some good choices are parsley, basil, oregano and thyme. Because long cooking can dull the flavor of dried herbs, add them about 20 minutes before the soup is done.

Lynne McKaige, *Savage, MN*

Beef Barley Soup

Delicious and satisfying! I like to use a heaping tablespoon of beef soup base instead of bouillon for a much richer beef flavor.

Makes 4 to 6 servings

2 c. carrots, peeled and thinly sliced
1 c. celery, thinly sliced
3/4 c. green pepper, diced
1 c. onion, diced
1 lb. stew beef cubes
1/2 c. pearled barley, uncooked
1/4 c. fresh parsley, chopped
3 cubes beef bouillon
2 T. catsup
1 t. salt
3/4 t. dried basil
5 c. water

Layer vegetables, beef and barley in a slow cooker; add seasonings. Pour water over all; do not stir. Cover and cook on low setting for 8 to 10 hours.

Sonia Hawkins, *Amarillo, TX*

Pig-in-a-Poke Ham Soup

A tasty use for the bone left over from a holiday ham! Or get a smoked ham hock at the butcher's counter.

Makes 10 servings

4 14-1/2 oz. cans green beans
1 meaty ham bone
4 potatoes, peeled and quartered
1 onion, sliced
pepper to taste

In a slow cooker, combine undrained green beans and remaining ingredients. Cover and cook on high setting for one hour. Reduce to low setting; cover and cook for 6 to 7 hours, until the meat falls off the bone. Remove ham bone; dice meat and return to slow cooker.

Kathy McCann-Neff, *Claxton, GA*

Chill-Chaser Pork Stew

After a day of raking leaves, this stew warms and rejuvenates you!

Serves 6

2 to 2-1/2 lbs. pork steaks, cubed
2 T. olive oil
2 sweet onions, chopped
2 green peppers, chopped
2 cloves garlic, minced
salt and pepper to taste
6-oz. can tomato paste
28-oz. can diced tomatoes
2 8-oz. cans sliced mushrooms, drained

In a Dutch oven over medium heat, sauté pork in oil until browned. Add onions, green peppers, garlic, salt and pepper. Cover; cook over medium-low heat until pork is tender. Add tomato paste, tomatoes with juice and mushrooms; bring to a boil. Reduce heat to low; simmer for one hour, stirring often.

Chill-Chaser Pork Stew

Chicken Corn Chowder

Katie French, *Portland, TX*

Chicken Corn Chowder

A quick main dish that goes great with a big, buttery piece of cornbread.

Serves 6 to 8

1-1/2 c. milk
10-1/2 oz. can chicken broth
10-3/4 oz. can cream of chicken soup
10-3/4 oz. can cream of potato soup
1 to 2 10-oz. cans chicken, drained
1/3 c. green onion, chopped
11-oz. can sweet corn & diced peppers
4-oz. can chopped green chiles, drained
8-oz. pkg. shredded Cheddar cheese

Mix together all ingredients except cheese in a stockpot. Cook over low heat, stirring frequently, for 15 minutes, or until heated through. Add cheese; stir until melted.

Flavor Booster

∙∙∙∙∙∙∙∙∙∙∙∙∙ ✳ ∙∙∙∙∙∙∙∙∙∙∙∙∙

A toasty touch for soups! Butter bread slices and cut into shapes using mini cookie cutters. Bake on a baking sheet at 425 degrees until crisp, then garnish filled soup bowls before serving.

Marlene Strobel, *Perry Hall, MD*

Fisherman's Wharf Stew

Vary this savory stew by adding other seafood like red snapper and crabmeat.

Makes 6 servings

2 T. olive oil
1 c. leek, sliced
2 cloves garlic, finely chopped
1 c. baby carrots, thinly sliced
6 roma tomatoes, quartered and sliced
1/2 c. green pepper, chopped
1/2 t. fennel seed
1 bay leaf
8-oz. bottle clam juice
1 c. dry white wine or water
1 lb. cod, sliced 1-inch thick and cubed
1/2 lb. medium shrimp, peeled and cleaned
1 t. sugar
1 t. dried basil
1/2 t. salt
1/4 t. hot pepper sauce
2 T. fresh parsley, chopped

Mix oil, leek and garlic in a slow cooker. Add vegetables, fennel seed, bay leaf, clam juice and wine or water; stir. Cover and cook on low setting for 8 to 9 hours, until vegetables are tender. About 20 minutes before serving, gently stir in remaining ingredients except parsley. Cover and cook on high setting for 15 to 20 minutes, until fish flakes easily with a fork. Discard bay leaf; stir in parsley.

Virginia Watson, *Scranton, PA*

New England Clam Chowder

Once you taste this, you'll never go back to canned chowder!

Makes 6 servings

1/2 c. butter, melted
2 T. onion powder
2 t. dried thyme
2 stalks celery, chopped
46-oz. can clam juice
2 cubes chicken bouillon
2 bay leaves
3 16-oz. cans whole potatoes, drained and diced
3 10-oz. cans whole baby clams
2 c. light cream
2 c. milk
salt and pepper to taste

In a 7-quart slow cooker, stir together butter, onion powder, thyme and celery; cook on high setting for 30 minutes. Add clam juice, bouillon, bay leaves and potatoes. Cover and continue cooking on high setting for 2 hours. Add clams and their juice; turn setting to low and cook for an additional 2 hours. Stir in cream and milk; cook for an additional one hour, or until heated through. Before serving, discard bay leaves; add salt and pepper to taste.

Jeanne Dinnel, *Canby, OR*

Chicken Enchilada Soup

This recipe may look lengthy, but it goes together in a jiffy! Serve it with a simple salad of ripe tomato and avocado drizzled with lime vinaigrette dressing.

Serves 6

1 onion, chopped
1 clove garlic, pressed
1 to 2 t. oil
14-1/2 oz. can beef broth
14-1/2 oz. can chicken broth
10-3/4 oz. can cream of chicken soup
1-1/2 c. water
12-1/2 oz. can chicken, drained
4-oz. can chopped green chiles
2 t. Worcestershire sauce
1 T. steak sauce
1 t. ground cumin
1 t. chili powder
1/8 t. pepper
6 corn tortillas, cut into strips
1 c. shredded Cheddar cheese

In a stockpot over medium heat, sauté onion and garlic in oil. Add remaining ingredients except tortilla strips and cheese; bring to a boil. Cover; reduce heat and simmer for one hour, stirring occasionally. Uncover; stir in tortilla strips and cheese. Simmer an additional 10 minutes.

Chicken Enchilada Soup

Chili Stew

Linda Marshall, *Ontario, Canada*

Chili Stew

I planned to make chili, only to discover that I had no chili powder. So I put this together instead, and now it's our favorite.

Serves 6

1/2 onion, chopped
1/2 red pepper, chopped
1/2 yellow pepper, chopped
1 butternut squash, peeled and cubed
2 T. oil
1 T. garlic, chopped
1 lb. ground beef
1 T. smoked paprika
2 t. ground cumin
2 t. dried basil
2 t. dried thyme
1/8 to 1/4 t. Worcestershire sauce
28-oz. can plum tomatoes
28-oz. can diced tomatoes
15-1/2 oz. can kidney beans, drained and rinsed
15-1/2 oz. can black beans, drained and rinsed
2 T. all-purpose flour
2 c. beef broth
salt and pepper to taste

In a stockpot, cook onion, peppers and squash in oil until tender. Add garlic and beef. Cook until beef is browned; drain. Add spices, Worcestershire sauce, tomatoes with juice and beans; break up tomatoes with a spoon. In a bowl, mix flour and broth; stir into chili. Bring to a boil. Reduce heat, cover and simmer for 30 minutes to 2 hours. Season with salt and pepper.

John Zahn, *Hermansville, MI*

Mixed-Up Stew

Chicken and beef together...it's surprisingly tasty!

Makes 6 to 8 servings

1/4 c. red steak sauce
1/2 c. hot water
2 cubes chicken bouillon
1 t. sugar
1 t. salt
1/2 t. pepper
2 to 3 lbs. boneless, skinless chicken thighs
1 lb. stew beef, cut into 1-1/2 inch cubes
1 onion, chopped
2 potatoes, peeled and cubed
2 carrots, peeled and thinly sliced
16-oz. can stewed tomatoes
1/4 c. all-purpose flour

Combine steak sauce, water, bouillon, sugar, salt and pepper in a slow cooker; stir well. Add remaining ingredients except flour; mix carefully. Cover and cook on low setting for 7 to 10 hours, or on high setting for 4 hours, adding a little water if needed. Make a smooth paste of flour and 1/4 cup of liquid from stew; stir into slow cooker. Cover and cook on high setting until thickened.

Roberta Simpkins, *Mentor-on-the-Lake, OH*

Creamy Potato Soup

Garnish with a sprinkle of snipped fresh chives.

Serves 6

6 potatoes, peeled and cubed
2 onions, chopped
1 carrot, peeled and sliced
1 stalk celery, sliced
4 cubes chicken bouillon
1 T. dried parsley
5 c. water
1/4 t. pepper
1 T. salt
1/3 c. butter, melted
12-oz. can evaporated milk

Combine all ingredients except evaporated milk in a slow cooker. Cover and cook on low setting for 10 to 12 hours, or on high setting for 3 to 4 hours. Stir in milk during last hour of cooking.

Lisa Purcell, *Ontario, Canada*

Clam & Scallop Chowder

For a special presentation, serve this steaming chowder in hollowed-out rounds of sourdough bread... oh-so good!

Serves 4

2 onions, finely chopped
1/4 c. butter, divided
1 t. salt
1 t. pepper
1 c. chicken broth or water
2 potatoes, peeled and cubed
1/4 lb. bay scallops
10-oz. can baby clams, drained and 1/2 c. liquid reserved
1 c. light cream
1 c. milk
2 slices bacon, crisply cooked and crumbled

In a large heavy saucepan over medium heat, cook onions in 2 tablespoons butter for 5 minutes, or until tender. Add salt, pepper, broth or water and potatoes; cook until fork-tender. Reduce heat; add scallops and cook just until tender, 4 to 5 minutes. Stir in clams with reserved liquid, cream, milk, bacon and remaining butter. Heat through without boiling for 3 minutes, or until hot.

Handy Tip

·············· ✳ ··············

A vintage covered soup tureen does double duty at a casual dinner of soup & sandwiches. It keeps the soup hot and tasty while also serving as a centerpiece.

Clam & Scallop Chowder

Kitchen Cabinet Mild White Chili

Becky Hall, *Belton, MO*

Kitchen Cabinet Mild White Chili

This recipe was created on a cold night with ingredients from the kitchen cabinet. It can easily be spiced up with a can of diced chiles or chopped jalapeño peppers.

Makes 4 servings

2 15-1/2 oz. cans Great Northern beans
Optional: 4-1/2 oz. can diced green chiles
14-oz. can chicken broth
1 T. dried, minced onion
1 T. red pepper flakes
1-1/2 t. dried, minced garlic
1 t. ground cumin
1/2 t. dried oregano
1/8 t. cayenne pepper
1/8 t. ground cloves
1-1/2 c. cooked chicken, chopped
4-oz. can sliced mushrooms, drained
1 c. shredded sharp Cheddar cheese

In a Dutch oven, combine all ingredients except chicken, mushrooms and cheese. Cook over medium heat for 5 minutes; bring to a boil. Reduce heat and simmer 5 minutes. Add chicken and mushrooms; simmer, uncovered, for 8 to 10 minutes, until heated through. Serve with cheese.

Handy Tip

Adapt a family favorite soup, stew or chili to make in a slow cooker. A recipe that simmers for 2 hours on the stovetop can usually cook all day on the low setting without overcooking.

Kimberly Wacht, *Tuba City, AZ*

Lazy-Day Soup

Sometimes I mix up the ingredients for this soup the night before, refrigerate and pop in the slow cooker in the morning. Delicious!

Serves 4 to 6

28-oz. pkg. frozen diced potatoes with onion and peppers
3 14-1/2 oz. cans chicken broth
16-oz. jar pasteurized process cheese sauce
10-3/4 oz. can cream of celery soup
1 to 2 c. diced cooked ham or Polish sausage, diced

Mix together all ingredients in slow cooker. Cover and cook on low setting for 6 to 8 hours, or on high setting for 3 hours.

Eleanor Paternoster, *Bridgeport, CT*

Eleanor's Lentil Stew

Jazz up this down-home stew with a swirl of pesto.

Serves 8

16-oz. pkg. dried lentils
4 c. water
3 c. cooked ham, diced
2 c. celery, chopped
2 c. carrots, peeled and chopped
2 10-1/2 oz. cans chicken broth

Combine all ingredients in a slow cooker. Cover and cook on low setting for 7 to 9 hours.

Betty Lou Wright, *Hendersonville, TN*

BBQ Sloppy Joe Soup

This recipe was a happy accident! One day I made vegetable soup. Remembering leftover Sloppy Joe sauce in the fridge, I stirred it into the soup. What a hit!

Makes 6 to 8 servings

1 lb. ground beef chuck
16-oz. can barbecue Sloppy Joe sauce
10-3/4 oz. can cream of potato soup
10-3/4 oz. can minestrone soup
1-1/4 c. water
15-oz. can light red kidney beans, drained and rinsed
14-1/2 oz. can green beans, drained
15-1/4 oz. can green peas, drained
15-oz. can diced tomatoes, drained
garlic powder and steak seasoning to taste
Garnish: oyster crackers

In a large saucepan over medium heat, brown beef; drain. Stir in Sloppy Joe sauce; heat through. Add remaining ingredients except crackers; simmer until bubbly, about 10 to 15 minutes. Serve with crackers.

BBQ Sloppy Joe Soup

Hungarian Mushroom Soup

Carleen Pettit, Sidney, OH

Hungarian Mushroom Soup

My family loves this creamy dish. It's so different from the typical soup.

Makes 8 to 10 servings

1/4 c. onion, diced
8 c. sliced mushrooms
1 c. butter
1 c. all-purpose flour
2 16-oz. cans chicken broth
3 T. paprika
1/4 c. soy sauce
16-oz. container sour cream
1 T. dried parsley
1 T. dill weed
2 T. lemon juice
12-oz. can evaporated milk

In a stockpot over medium heat, sauté onion and mushrooms in butter until tender. Stir in flour. Add remaining ingredients except evaporated milk; bring to a simmer. Stir in evaporated milk. Cover and simmer over low heat about one hour.

Nancy Willis, Farmington Hills, MI

Tortellini-Sausage Soup

Your family will love this hearty, savory soup. Toss a crisp green salad and pop some garlic bread in the oven...dinner is served!

Makes 10 to 12 servings

1 lb. ground Italian pork sausage
1 c. onion, chopped
2 cloves garlic, minced
4 c. beef broth
1/2 c. dry red wine or beef broth
28-oz. can crushed tomatoes
28-oz. can diced tomatoes
15-oz. can tomato sauce
1 c. carrots, peeled and chopped
1/2 t. dried basil
1/2 t. dried oregano
1 T. dried parsley
1 c. zucchini, chopped
9-oz. pkg. refrigerated cheese tortellini, uncooked

Brown sausage in a large stockpot over medium heat; drain. Add onion and garlic; sauté until tender. Stir in broth, wine or broth, tomatoes with their juice, tomato sauce, carrots and herbs. Bring to a boil; stir well. Reduce heat; cover and simmer for 30 minutes. Stir in zucchini and tortellini; cover and simmer for an additional 15 minutes.

Sally Burke, *Lansing, MI*

Slow-Simmered Split Pea Soup

A scrumptious use for leftover baked ham! If you have a ham bone, add it to the pot right at the beginning for extra flavor.

Makes 6 servings

16-oz. pkg. dried split green peas
1/4 c. dried split yellow peas
3 qts. water
1 onion, chopped
2 T. chicken bouillon granules
1/4 to 1/2 t. pepper
1 bay leaf
3/4 lb. cooked ham, finely chopped
1-1/2 c. carrots, peeled and thinly sliced
1 c. celery, chopped
1 potato, peeled and cubed

In a large soup pot, combine dried peas, water, onion, bouillon, pepper and bay leaf. Simmer over low heat, uncovered, for 1-1/2 to 2 hours. Add remaining ingredients. Cook for an additional 1-1/2 to 2 hours, stirring occasionally, until peas and vegetables are tender and desired thickness is reached. Discard bay leaf before serving.

Stephanie Swensen, *Mapleton, UT*

Mom's Creamy Chicken Chowder

Paired with homemade bread or rolls, this is my family's most-requested soup.

Serves 12 to 15

4 to 6 boneless, skinless chicken breasts, cubed
3 c. potatoes, peeled and cubed
12 c. chicken broth
3 cubes chicken bouillon
1 c. celery, diced
1/2 c. onion, diced
1-1/2 c. carrot, peeled and grated
1/2 c. butter
12-oz. can evaporated milk
1/2 c. water
1-1/2 c. all-purpose flour

Combine chicken, potatoes, broth, bouillon, celery, onion and carrot in a large pot. Simmer over medium heat until chicken is cooked and vegetables are tender. Stir in butter until melted; set aside. In a blender, process milk, water and flour until smooth; add to soup mixture. Cook and stir until thickened.

Mom's Creamy Chicken Chowder

Chicken Taco Soup

Janet Allen, *Hauser, ID*

Chicken Taco Soup

A spicy and flavorful soup...serve this favorite with bandannas for napkins and a bottle of hot pepper sauce for those who like it fiery!

Serves 8

1 onion, chopped
16-oz. can chili beans
15-oz. can black beans
15-oz. can corn
2 10-oz. cans diced tomatoes with green chiles
8-oz. can tomato sauce
12-oz. can regular or non-alcoholic beer
1-1/4 oz. pkg. taco seasoning mix
3 boneless, skinless chicken breasts
Garnish: shredded Cheddar cheese, crushed
   tortilla chips
Optional: sour cream

In a slow cooker, mix together onion, beans, corn, diced tomatoes with juice, tomato sauce and beer. Add seasoning mix; stir to blend. Lightly press chicken breasts into mixture in slow cooker until partially covered. Cover and cook on low setting for 5 hours. Remove chicken from slow cooker; shred and return to soup. Cover and cook for an additional 2 hours. Top servings of soup with cheese, crushed chips and sour cream, if desired.

Emily Edwards, *Alliance, OH*

Tom Turkey Noodle Soup

A family tradition for Thanksgiving weekend.

Serves 4 to 6

2 18-1/2 oz. cans turkey broth
4-2/3 c. water
1 T. dried parsley
1 t. dried, minced onion
4 c. cooked turkey, diced
8-oz. pkg. kluski egg noodles, uncooked

Combine broth, water, parsley and onion in a large stockpot over medium heat; bring to a boil. Add turkey and noodles; reduce heat and simmer for 10 to 15 minutes.

Carol Donnelly, *San Bernardino, CA*

Classic French Onion Soup

This delicious restaurant favorite is easy to make at home.

Makes 4 servings

3 T. olive oil
3 sweet onions, thinly sliced
3 14-1/2 oz. cans beef broth
1/2 t. salt
4 thick slices French bread, toasted
1 c. Gruyère or Swiss cheese, shredded

Heat oil in a large saucepan over medium heat. Add onions and cook until lightly golden. Reduce heat; cook for 30 to 40 minutes until deep golden, stirring frequently. Add broth and salt. Reduce heat to low; simmer for 15 to 20 minutes. Ladle soup into 4 oven-proof bowls; top each bowl with a toasted bread slice and sprinkle with cheese. Broil 4 inches from heat for 2 to 3 minutes, until cheese is bubbly and lightly golden.

Rebecca Ross, *Topeka, KS*

Smoky Sausage & 2-Bean Soup

I started making minestrone and got carried away trying to create a hearty soup for a cold day! This is what came out, and its flavor just can't be beat.

Makes 8 to 10 servings

1 lb. smoked pork sausage, sliced
15-oz. can tomato sauce
2 14-1/2 oz. cans low-sodium beef broth
15-oz. can pinto beans, drained and rinsed
15-oz. can kidney beans, drained and rinsed
1/4 c. onion, chopped
1/4 c. celery, chopped
1/4 c. green pepper, chopped
1/4 c. red pepper, chopped
1 c. water
2 cubes beef bouillon
1/2 t. pepper
1/4 t. garlic salt
1/2 t. Italian seasoning
1 to 2 c. cooked rice

Combine all ingredients except rice in a slow cooker. Cover and cook on low setting for 6 to 8 hours. About 30 minutes before serving, stir in rice. Cover and cook remaining 30 minutes.

Flavor Booster
·······················* ·······················
Add a tangy twist to bean soup by drizzling some balsamic vinegar in while it simmers.

Smoky Sausage & 2-Bean Soup

Brunswick Stew

Jennie Gist, Gooseberry Patch

Brunswick Stew

This hearty stew is a fall and wintertime favorite around our house. I usually serve big bowls of it with a mug of hot cider.

Serves 6

3-lb. boneless pork shoulder roast, quartered
3 redskin potatoes, diced
1 onion, chopped
28-oz. can crushed tomatoes
18-oz. bottle favorite barbecue sauce
14-oz. can chicken broth
9-oz. pkg. frozen baby lima beans, thawed
9-oz. pkg. frozen corn, thawed
6 T. brown sugar, packed
1 t. salt
Garnish: saltine crackers

Stir together all ingredients except crackers in a slow cooker. Cover and cook on high setting for 6 hours, or until pork and potatoes are tender. Remove pork with a slotted spoon; shred. Return pork to slow cooker; stir well. Ladle stew into bowls; serve with crackers.

Rose Cannon, Gordon, AL

Rose's Cream of Potato Soup

Garnish this thick, cheesy soup with snipped chives.

Makes 4 to 6 servings

1/2 onion, chopped
1/4 c. butter
8 potatoes, peeled and cubed
2 t. roasted garlic & red bell pepper seasoning blend
salt and pepper to taste
10-3/4 oz. can cream of chicken soup
1 c. shredded mozzarella cheese
1 c. shredded Parmesan cheese
1/2 c. Colby cheese, shredded
2 to 2-1/2 c. milk

In a large saucepan over medium heat, sauté onion in butter. Add potatoes and enough water to cover; stir in seasonings. Cook until potatoes break apart with a fork. Stir in soup; add cheeses and stir until melted. Stir in milk to desired thickness; adjust seasoning. Cook, stirring occasionally, for a few more minutes until thickened.

Carie VanCleave, *Abilene, TX*

Easy Taco Soup

One day I was so hungry for soup. I found some canned beans, tomatoes and corn in the pantry, added a few other ingredients and made a fantastic soup...my family loves it! Garnish it with shredded cheese and crushed tortilla chips.

Serves 8

1 lb. ground beef
14-1/2 oz. can beef broth
16-oz. can pinto beans
16-oz. can black beans
15-1/4 oz. can corn
10-oz. can diced tomatoes with chiles
1 yellow squash, chopped
1 zucchini, chopped
2 c. water
1-1/4 oz. pkg. taco seasoning mix
1-oz. pkg. ranch salad dressing mix
2 T. fresh cilantro, chopped
salt and pepper to taste

In a large stockpot over medium heat, cook ground beef until browned; drain. Stir in remaining ingredients. Reduce heat and simmer until squash and zucchini are tender, about 15 minutes.

Staci Meyers, *Cocoa, FL*

3-Bean Ravioli Minestrone

A meatless main dish that's good and good for you... replace the chicken broth with vegetable broth if you wish.

Makes 4 to 6 servings

1 onion, chopped
2 carrots, peeled and chopped
2 stalks celery, sliced
2 cloves garlic, minced
1 T. olive oil
3 14-1/2 oz. cans chicken broth
10-oz. pkg. frozen baby lima beans
15-oz. can kidney beans, drained and rinsed
15-1/2 oz. can garbanzo beans, drained and rinsed
2 14-1/2 oz. cans diced tomatoes
2 t. Italian seasoning
1/2 t. salt
1 t. pepper
7-oz. pkg. mini cheese ravioli, cooked

Combine onion, carrots, celery, garlic and olive oil in a large stockpot. Sauté over medium-high heat for 10 minutes, or until tender, stirring often. Add broth, beans, tomatoes and seasonings. Reduce heat to medium; simmer for 20 minutes. Stir in cooked ravioli just before serving.

3-Bean Ravioli Minestrone

Chorizo & Potato Stew

Angela Murphey, *Tempe, AZ*

Chorizo & Potato Stew

If your supermarket doesn't have Mexican chorizo sausage, mild or spicy Italian sausage will work equally well.

Serves 8

2 onions, diced
2 red peppers, diced
1 T. garlic, minced
2 bay leaves
2 T. olive oil
salt to taste
3-1/2 lbs. new potatoes, cubed
1 lb. chorizo sausage, sliced
4 c. chicken broth
1/2 c. water
1-1/2 t. paprika
1/2 t. red pepper flakes
1 t. pepper
2 T. fresh parsley, minced

Sauté onions, peppers, garlic and bay leaves in olive oil for 2 to 3 minutes in a large soup pot. Add salt to taste; continue cooking, covered, over low heat for 15 minutes. Add potatoes and sausage; sauté for 2 minutes over medium heat. Add broth, water, paprika, red pepper flakes and pepper. Bring to a boil; reduce heat to medium and continue cooking, uncovered, for 20 minutes. Add parsley; continue cooking for 10 to 15 minutes, until potatoes are tender. Cover and let stand for 5 minutes. Discard bay leaves before serving.

Melissa Harrell, *Wahoo, NE*

Easy Chicken Noodle Soup

My family loves chicken noodle soup, but I don't always have time to make homemade soup from scratch, starting with making the broth. This is really easy...a great meal for a chilly autumn night!

Serves 6

2 14-1/2 oz. cans chicken broth
2 10-3/4 oz. cans cream of chicken soup
6 c. water
12-1/2 oz. can chicken, drained
2 cubes chicken bouillon
1/2 c. celery, diced
1/4 c. carrot, peeled and thinly sliced
1/2 to 1 t. lemon pepper, dill weed or seasoned
   salt, as desired
8-oz. pkg. wide egg noodles, uncooked

Combine broth, soup and water in a medium soup kettle; stir until well blended. Add chicken, bouillon cubes, celery, carrot and desired seasoning. Bring to a boil over medium heat, stirring occasionally. Turn down to medium-low heat; add noodles and stir. Cook for an additional 10 to 15 minutes, until noodles are tender, stirring occasionally to keep noodles from sticking.

Sherry Saarinen, Hancock, MI

Finnish Sweet Potato Soup

Sweet potatoes grow abundantly here in the Upper Peninsula of Michigan. I've found a lot of uses for them, but none is as tasty as this soup!

Makes about 4 servings

3 sweet potatoes, peeled and sliced
2 c. chicken broth
1-1/2 c. light cream or half-and-half
1 t. sugar
1/8 t. ground cloves
1/8 t. nutmeg
salt to taste
Optional: sour cream, nutmeg

Put sweet potatoes and broth in a slow cooker. Cover and cook on high setting for 2 to 3 hours, until potatoes are tender. Purée in a blender or food processor. Return puréed potatoes to slow cooker; add remaining ingredients. Cover and cook on high setting for an additional one to 2 hours. Serve hot or chilled with a dollop of sour cream and a sprinkle of nutmeg, if desired.

Debi Piper, *Vicksburg, MI*

Chicken Stew Over Biscuits

One of my family's favorites...my husband and kids always come back for seconds! Very warm and comforting.

Makes 4 to 6 servings

2 c. water
3/4 c. white wine or chicken broth
2 .87-oz. pkgs. chicken gravy mix
2 cloves garlic, minced
1 T. fresh parsley, minced
1 to 2 t. chicken bouillon granules
1/2 t. pepper
5 carrots, peeled and cut into 1-inch pieces
1 onion, cut into 8 wedges
4 skinless, boneless chicken breasts, cut into
  bite-size pieces
3 T. all-purpose flour
1/3 c. cold water
16.3-oz. tube refrigerated large buttermilk
  biscuits, baked

Combine first 7 ingredients in a slow cooker; mix until blended. Add carrots, onion and chicken; cover and cook on low setting for 7 to 8 hours. In a small bowl, stir together flour and cold water until smooth; gradually stir into slow cooker. Increase setting to high; cover and cook for one hour. Place biscuits in soup bowls; top with stew.

Finnish Sweet Potato Soup

Minnesota Wild Rice Soup

Jo Ann, *Gooseberry Patch*

Hearty Vegetable-Beef Soup

Everyone needs a great chilly-day recipe for veggie beef soup, and this is mine! On busy days, I'll use a slow cooker. Combine the browned beef and onion with everything else except the peas and herbs, cover and cook on low for 8 to 10 hours. Stir in the peas and herbs half an hour before dinner is served.

Makes 4 servings

1 lb. stew beef cubes
1 onion, chopped
1 T. oil
4 c. beef broth
3 c. water
14-1/2 oz. can crushed tomatoes
1 c. carrots, peeled and sliced
1-1/2 c. potatoes, peeled and cubed
1 c. celery, sliced
1 c. green beans, sliced
1/2 c. corn
1/2 c. frozen peas
1/2 t. dried basil
1/2 t. dried oregano

In a stockpot over medium heat, cook beef and onion in oil until beef is browned. Add broth, water, tomatoes and their juice. Reduce heat and simmer until beef is nearly tender, about 1-1/2 hours. Add carrots, potatoes, celery, green beans and corn; continue to simmer another 30 minutes. Stir in frozen peas and herbs; simmer just until peas are tender.

Margaret Haase, *Lake City, MN*

Minnesota Wild Rice Soup

This soup's flavor is even better if made a day ahead, refrigerated overnight and reheated.

Makes 10 to 12 servings

6 T. butter
1/2 c. onion, chopped
1 c. sliced mushrooms
1/2 c. all-purpose flour
3 c. chicken broth
1/2 c. wild rice, cooked
3 c. cooked ham, diced
1/2 c. carrots, peeled and grated
1/2 c. slivered almonds
1 c. half-and-half

Melt butter in a large saucepan over medium heat. Add onion and mushrooms; cook until tender. Blend in flour; gradually add broth. Cook and stir constantly until broth comes to a boil. Stir in rice, ham, carrots and almonds; simmer for 5 minutes. Add half-and-half; heat through without boiling.

Shelly McMurtrey, *Rison, AR*

Beefy Nacho Cheese Soup

Stir up this hearty soup in a jiffy for your hungry family...it has just five ingredients!

Serves 6

1 lb. ground beef
2 c. beef broth
8-oz. jar picante sauce
1/8 t. ground cumin
10-3/4 oz. can nacho cheese soup

In a large saucepan over medium heat, brown ground beef; drain. Add broth, picante sauce and cumin; bring to a boil. Reduce heat; cover and simmer for 15 minutes, stirring frequently. Stir in cheese soup; gently heat through without boiling.

Cindy Amice, *Mechanicsburg, PA*

Autumn Beef Barley Soup

Teriyaki sauce is the surprise ingredient in this tasty soup.

Makes 4 servings

1 lb. ground beef
1/2 c. onion, chopped
3 cloves garlic, minced
8-oz. pkg. sliced mushrooms
1/2 t. dried basil
garlic salt to taste
salt and pepper to taste
3 c. water
1 c. beef broth
1/4 c. teriyaki sauce
1 T. balsamic vinegar
1 c. carrots, peeled and chopped
1 c. potatoes, peeled and chopped
1/2 c. celery, chopped
16-oz. can diced tomatoes
1/2 c. catsup
1/2 c. pearled barley, uncooked

Place ground beef, onion, garlic and mushrooms in a large pot; sprinkle with seasonings. Cook over medium heat until beef is browned; drain. Add remaining ingredients except barley; bring to a boil. Stir in barley; reduce heat and simmer for 30 minutes to one hour.

Beefy Nacho Cheese Soup

The Great Pumpkin C

Kelly Durocher, *Schenectady, NY*

The Great Pumpkin Chili

I won a chili contest through my local newspaper with this recipe. The pumpkin adds great flavor and makes the chili very creamy. My girls love this chili...I hope you enjoy it too!

Makes 12 servings

3 lbs. ground beef
3 14-1/2 oz. cans diced tomatoes
2 15-oz. cans kidney beans, drained and rinsed
15-oz. can pumpkin
2 green peppers, chopped
2 onions, chopped
2 T. chili powder
2 T. honey
1/4 t. cayenne pepper
1 t. salt

Brown ground beef in a large pot over medium heat, stirring to crumble; drain. Stir in remaining ingredients; reduce heat to low. Simmer, covered, for one to 2 hours, adding water as necessary.

Flavor Booster

* * * * * * * * * * * ✳ * * * * * * * * * * *

A terrific way to "beef up" any recipe...cut roast beef into bite-size pieces, season to taste and toss into casseroles, soups and sauces.

Regan Reeves, *Panama, IL*

Mom's Chilly-Day Cheese Soup

My mom always made this soup when the weather turned cold. Now I make it for my family...they love it too!

Makes 4 to 6 servings

8 potatoes, peeled and diced
1 onion, chopped
2 qts. water
2 16-oz. pkgs. frozen broccoli, cauliflower and carrot blend
10-3/4 oz. can cream of celery soup
10-3/4 oz. can cream of chicken soup
16-oz. pkg. pasteurized process cheese spread, cubed

Combine potatoes, onion and water in a large saucepan. Bring to a boil over medium-high heat. Reduce heat and simmer until tender, 15 to 20 minutes. Add frozen vegetables; cook until tender, about 12 to 15 minutes. Stir in soups; mix well. Add cheese and simmer for a few more minutes, until cheese is melted.

Chapter three

Dinners in the Oven

Gather 'round...dinner is served! Filled with recipes baked bubbly and delicious in the oven, you'll find everything from Summery Herbed Tomato Pie to Sweet & Smoky Chicken. There are go-to comfort favorites like Turkey Tetrazzini and Puffy Potato Casserole, and easy-to-fix dishes like Crustless Pizza Quiche and Cheesy Baked Tortellini. Give the Country-Style Turkey Pot Roast a try, it's a real winner!

Laurie Aitken, *Walden, NY*

Easy Beef Burgundy

A simple-to-make version of this classic dish...great for company.

Serves 6 to 8

2 lbs. stew beef cubes
2 10-3/4 oz. cans cream of mushroom soup
2 4-oz. cans mushrooms, drained
2 c. red wine or beef broth
1-1/2 oz. pkg. onion soup mix
3 to 4 c. prepared egg noodles

Combine all ingredients except noodles in a 2-quart casserole dish. Cover and bake at 350 degrees for 3 hours, stirring occasionally. Serve over prepared noodles.

Amy Hunt, *Traphill, NC*

Crustless Pizza Quiche

This quiche goes well with a salad for a quick supper.

Serves 4 to 6

1/2 c. pepperoni, diced
8-oz. can sliced mushrooms, drained
5 eggs, beaten
3/4 c. milk
1/8 t. dried oregano
1/8 t. dried basil
8-oz. pkg. shredded mozzarella cheese

Layer pepperoni and mushrooms in a greased 9" pie plate. In a bowl, whisk together eggs, milk and seasonings; pour over pepperoni and mushrooms. Top with cheese. Bake, uncovered, at 400 degrees for 20 to 25 minutes, until golden and heated through.

Tina Stidam, *Delaware, OH*

Country-Style Turkey Pot Roast

This pot roast makes its own delicious thick gravy. The recipe works well with other meats too.

Serves 8 to 10

2 to 3 T. oil
6 to 8-lb. skinless turkey breast
salt to taste
6 potatoes, peeled and quartered
6 to 8 carrots, peeled and halved
3 turnips, peeled and quartered
2 stalks celery, quartered
2 onions, halved
1/2 head cabbage, quartered
2 3-oz. pkgs. brown gravy mix
1-1/2 oz. pkg. onion soup mix
2-1/4 c. water

Heat oil in a roaster pan over medium heat; add turkey breast and sauté on all sides until golden. Sprinkle with salt to taste. Add vegetables to roaster; set aside. Combine gravy and soup mixes with water; pour over turkey and vegetables. Cover and bake at 350 degrees for 2 to 3 hours, depending on size of breast, basting with pan juices after 1-1/2 hours.

> ~ *Handy Tip* ~
>
> A pizza cutter is ideal for dividing up slices of quiche while it's still in the pie plate.

Crustless Pizza Quiche

Chicken-Broccoli Divan

Tiffany Mayberry, *Harriman, TN*

Chicken-Broccoli Divan

This is a delightful recipe I remember my mother cooking for me when I was a little girl.

Serves 4

2 c. cooked chicken, cubed
16-oz. pkg. frozen broccoli flowerets, thawed
2 10-3/4 oz. cans cream of chicken soup
3/4 c. mayonnaise
1 t. lemon juice
1/2 c. shredded Cheddar cheese

Place chicken in a greased 13"x9" baking pan. Layer broccoli on top. In a bowl, stir together soup, mayonnaise and lemon juice. Pour soup mixture over broccoli; top with cheese. Bake, uncovered, at 350 degrees for 45 minutes, or until bubbly.

J.J. Presley, *Portland, TX*

Cheesy Sausage-Potato Casserole

Add some fresh green beans too, if you like.

Serves 6 to 8

3 to 4 potatoes, sliced
1 lb. smoked pork sausage, sliced
1 onion, chopped
1/2 c. butter, sliced
1 c. shredded Cheddar cheese

Layer potatoes, sausage and onion in a 13"x9" baking pan sprayed with non-stick vegetable spray. Dot with butter; sprinkle with cheese. Bake, uncovered, at 350 degrees for 1-1/2 hours, or until potatoes are tender.

Pamela Bures Raybon, *Edna, TX*

Simple Tuna One-Dish

My teenage sons request this dish often...when I'm really busy, they cook it for all of us.

Serves 7 to 9

2 T. butter
1/2 c. onion, diced
2 T. all-purpose flour
1 c. milk
2 6-oz. cans tuna, drained
15-oz. can peas, drained
3/4 t. salt
1/4 t. pepper
8-oz. tube refrigerated biscuits

Melt butter over medium heat in a 1-1/2 quart casserole dish. Sauté onion until tender. Add flour and milk; stir well over low heat until smooth and thickened. Add tuna, peas, salt and pepper; mix well. Top with biscuits; bake at 425 degrees for 15 minutes, or until biscuits are golden.

Flavor Booster

Stewing chicken to use later in chicken salads or casseroles? Let it cool in its broth before cutting up...it will have twice the flavor.

Mary Kathryn Carter, *Platte City, MO*

Cream Cheese Enchiladas

This creamy variation on Mexican enchiladas is yummy! It won me 1st place in a local newspaper's holiday cooking contest.

Makes 8 servings

2 8-oz. pkgs. cream cheese, softened
1 c. sour cream
2 10-oz. cans mild green chile enchilada sauce
1/4 c. jalapeños, chopped
1 lb. ground beef, browned and drained
1/2 c. shredded sharp Cheddar cheese
1 sweet onion, chopped
1/2 c. sliced black olives
8 to 12 flour tortillas
Garnish: sliced black olives, chopped tomato, shredded
   lettuce, chopped green onion

In a large bowl, blend together cream cheese, sour cream, enchilada sauce and jalapeños; set aside. Combine ground beef and shredded cheese in another bowl; set aside. Fill each tortilla with one to 2 tablespoons cream cheese mixture and one to 2 tablespoons beef mixture. Sprinkle each with onion and olives; roll up tortillas. Place seam-side down in a 13"x9" baking pan; cover with remaining cream cheese mixture. Bake at 400 degrees for 30 to 40 minutes; cover if top begins to brown. Garnish with olives, tomato, lettuce and green onion.

Maggie Jo Tucker, *Hartsfield, GA*

Maggie's Kickin' King Ranch Chicken

I got this recipe from my dear friend Aunt B, but I have adapted it to fit our tastes!

Serves 8 to 10

5 to 6 boneless, skinless chicken breasts, cooked
   and cubed
2 10-3/4 oz. cans cream of chicken soup
2 10-3/4 oz. cans cream of mushroom soup
2 10-oz. cans diced tomatoes with green chiles
1 T. chili powder
2 t. garlic salt
1-1/3 c. water
salt and pepper to taste
2 18-oz. pkgs. restaurant-style tortilla chips, divided
2 12-oz. pkgs. shredded Cheddar cheese

In a large bowl, combine chicken and remaining ingredients except chips and cheese; mix well. Place chips in a single layer in the bottom and up the sides of an ungreased 15"x10" baking pan; reserve any remaining chips. Spoon chicken mixture over chips. Cover with cheese. Bake, uncovered, at 350 degrees for 30 minutes, or until bubbly. Serve with remaining chips.

Maggie's Kickin' King Ranch Chicken

Marilyn Morel, *Keene, NH*

Chicken & Asparagus Bake

A delicious casserole that's simple to prepare and bakes in under 45 minutes.

Serves 6 to 8

6 boneless, skinless chicken breasts, cooked and cubed
3 14-1/2 oz. cans asparagus pieces, drained
2-oz. jar chopped pimentos, drained
3/4 c. slivered almonds
3 10-3/4 oz. cans cream of mushroom soup
2 2.8-oz. cans French fried onions

Layer chicken, asparagus, pimentos, almonds and soup in a lightly greased 2-1/2 quart casserole dish. Cover with aluminum foil; bake at 350 degrees for 30 to 40 minutes, until bubbly. Uncover and top with onions. Bake for an additional 5 minutes.

Connie Hilty, *Pearland, TX*

Easy Sunday Chicken Dinner

This dinner is so simple to put in the oven before we leave for church...it's ready when we get back, and the house smells heavenly!

Serves 5 to 6

1 T. all-purpose flour
1 t. garlic salt, divided
1 lb. redskin potatoes
8-oz. pkg. baby carrots
2 stalks celery, sliced
1 onion, cut in wedges
4 to 5 lbs. chicken
1 T. oil
1 t. paprika

Shake flour and 1/2 teaspoon garlic salt in a large oven bag; place bag in a 13"x9" baking pan. Arrange vegetables in bag; turn to coat with flour. Push vegetables to outer edge of bag. Brush chicken with oil; sprinkle remaining garlic and paprika over chicken. Arrange chicken in bag in center of vegetables. Close bag with nylon tie provided; cut six, 1/2-inch slits in top of bag. Bake at 350 degrees for 1-1/2 hours, or until chicken juices run clear.

Peggy Buckshaw, *Stow, OH*

Peg's Tomato-Bacon Pie

This scrumptious pie will be a hit at your next get-together!

Serves 6 to 8

2 to 3 tomatoes, peeled and sliced
9-inch pie crust, baked
salt and pepper to taste
1/2 c. green onions, chopped
1/3 c. fresh basil, chopped
1/2 c. bacon, crisply cooked and crumbled
1 c. mayonnaise
1 c. shredded Cheddar cheese

Layer tomato slices in pie crust. Season to taste with salt and pepper. Top with onions, basil and bacon. In a bowl, mix together mayonnaise and cheese; spread over bacon. Bake, uncovered, at 350 degrees for 30 minutes, or until lightly golden.

Janice O'Brien, *Warrenton, VA*

Summery Herbed Tomato Pie

Refrigerated pie crust makes this one quick-to-fix meal.

Serves 8 to 10

9-inch pie crust
3 to 4 tomatoes, sliced
1/2 c. fresh chives, chopped
2 T. fresh basil, chopped
salt and pepper to taste
2 c. shredded mozzarella cheese
1/2 c. mayonnaise

Press pie crust into a 9" pie plate. Bake at 425 degrees for 5 minutes. Reduce oven to 400 degrees. Arrange tomato slices in crust; sprinkle with chives, basil, salt and pepper. Combine cheese and mayonnaise; spread over tomatoes. Bake at 400 degrees for 35 minutes.

Julie Brown, *Provo, UT*

Chicken-Zucchini Bake

This recipe proves there's no such thing as too many zucchini!

Serves 6 to 8

1 T. margarine, melted
12-oz. pkg. chicken-flavored stuffing mix
6 c. zucchini, sliced and steamed
1 c. carrots, peeled and grated
3 to 4 lbs. cooked chicken, diced
10-3/4 oz. can cream of chicken soup
1 c. sour cream
1/4 c. onion, chopped

Combine margarine and stuffing mix; spoon half of mixture in the bottom of a 13"x9" baking pan. Layer zucchini, carrots and chicken over the top; set aside. Mix soup, sour cream and onion together; spoon over chicken. Top with remaining stuffing mix; bake at 350 degrees for 45 minutes.

Simple Swap

Why not try a light substitution? Low-fat plain yogurt or cottage cheese is just as tasty as sour cream.

Amy Butcher, *Columbus, GA*

Easy Cheesy Ratatouille

When I first had this at a church potluck, I made sure to go back for seconds and to ask for the recipe!

Serves 6 to 8

1 eggplant, peeled and cut into 1-inch cubes
1 onion, diced
1 red pepper, diced
1 zucchini, cut into 1-inch cubes
1/4 c. sun-dried tomato vinaigrette
14-1/2 oz. can diced tomatoes
1/4 c. grated Parmesan cheese
1 c. shredded mozzarella cheese

Sauté vegetables with vinaigrette in a large oven-safe skillet over medium heat. Add tomatoes with juice; cook for 15 minutes. Sprinkle with cheeses. Bake, uncovered 350 degrees for 15 minutes, or until vegetables are tender.

Easy Cheesy Ratatouille

Mix all ingredients except noodles in a large bowl. Transfer to a greased 13"x9" baking pan. Cover and refrigerate overnight. Uncover and bake at 350 degrees for one hour, or until hot and bubbly. Top with noodles; return to oven for 5 minutes.

Kelly Alderson, *Erie, PA*

Fast & Fresh Asparagus Casserole

The crunch of water chestnuts sets this casserole apart.

Serves 6 to 8

1 lb. carrots, peeled, sliced and cooked
15-oz. can asparagus spears, drained
15-1/4 oz. can peas, drained
8-oz. can sliced water chestnuts, drained
3 eggs, hard-boiled, peeled and sliced
1/3 c. butter
10-3/4 oz. can cream of mushroom soup
1 c. shredded Cheddar cheese, divided
1 c. cracker crumbs
1/2 t. pepper

Layer carrots, asparagus and peas in a lightly greased 13"x9" baking pan. Place water chestnuts and sliced eggs over vegetables. Dot with butter. Mix soup and 3/4 cup cheese; spread over vegetable layers. Bake at 350 degrees for 30 minutes, or until bubbly. Sprinkle with crumbs, pepper and remaining cheese; bake an additional 5 minutes, or until cheese melts.

Betty Lou Wright, *Hendersonville, TN*

Alabama Chicken Casserole

If I had a nickel for every time this make-ahead casserole has been carried to a potluck, I'd be a wealthy woman!

Makes 10 to 12 servings

2 to 3 c. cooked chicken, chopped
4 eggs, hard-boiled, peeled and chopped
2 c. cooked rice
1-1/2 c. celery, chopped
1 onion, chopped
2 10-3/4 oz. cans cream of mushroom soup
1 c. mayonnaise
2 T. lemon juice
3-oz. pkg. slivered almonds
5-oz. can chow mein noodles

Debbi Corlew, *Colona, IL*

Quick Tuna Casserole

I grew up eating this meal, and it's still one of my all-time favorites.

Serves 4

2 6-oz. cans tuna, drained
10-3/4 oz. can cream of mushroom soup
3/4 c. milk
1 T. Worcestershire sauce
hot pepper sauce to taste
1 sleeve round buttery crackers, crushed

In a bowl, mix together all ingredients except crackers; set aside. In a greased 9"x9" baking pan, layer one-third of crackers and top with half of tuna mixture. Repeat layers; top with remaining crackers and more hot sauce, if desired. Bake, uncovered, at 350 degrees for 30 minutes, or until hot and bubbly.

— *Handy Tip* —

Add an extra can or 2 of soup, veggies or tuna to the grocery cart every week, then put aside these extras at home. Before you know it, you'll have a generous selection of canned goods for fall food drives.

Joann Britton, *Chesterfield, MO*

Chicken à la Kym

This recipe was my daughter's favorite recipe for company. I'm sending it in honor of her teenage daughter.

Makes 6 to 8 servings

4 boneless, skinless chicken breasts, halved
8 slices Swiss cheese
10-3/4 oz. can cream of chicken soup
1/4 c. white wine or chicken broth
1 c. chicken-flavored stuffing mix
1/4 c. butter, melted

Arrange chicken in a lightly greased 13"x9" baking pan; top with cheese slices. Combine soup, wine or broth and stuffing mix; spread over chicken. Drizzle with butter; bake at 350 degrees for 55 minutes.

Doris Reichard, *Baltimore, MD*

Baked Chicken Reuben

How clever...our favorite deli sandwich flavors in a casserole!

Serves 4

4 boneless, skinless chicken breasts
1/4 t. salt
1/8 t. pepper
2 c. sauerkraut, drained
8-oz. bottle Russian salad dressing
4 slices Swiss cheese
1 T. dried parsley
Garnish: fresh chives, chopped

Arrange chicken breasts in a greased 13"x9" baking pan; sprinkle with salt and pepper. Spread sauerkraut over chicken; pour dressing evenly over all. Top with cheese slices and parsley; cover and bake at 350 degrees for one hour, or until tender. Sprinkle with chives.

Debbie Hutchinson, *Spring, TX*

Cowpoke Casserole

A cast-iron skillet is perfect for this dish...it can go right into the oven to bake!

Serves 4 to 6

1 lb. ground beef
1/2 onion, chopped
salt and pepper to taste
1 t. chili powder
15-1/2 oz. can chili beans
8-oz. can tomato sauce
1/2 c. water
8-1/2 oz. pkg. cornbread mix
1/3 c. milk
1 egg, beaten

Brown beef with onion in an oven-proof skillet over medium heat. Drain; add salt and pepper to taste. Stir in chili powder, beans, tomato sauce and water. Simmer for 5 minutes; remove from heat. In a separate bowl, stir together cornbread mix, milk and egg; spoon over beef mixture and place skillet in oven. Bake, uncovered, at 350 degrees for 25 minutes, or until cornbread topping is golden and cooked through.

~ *Handy Tip* ~

Stock up at supermarket sales on large packages of ground beef, chicken or pork chops, then repackage into recipe-size portions before freezing.

Tori Willis, *Champaign, IL*

No-Muss Chicken Dinner

This easy recipe makes its own delicious chicken gravy.

Serves 6

1 T. all-purpose flour
10-3/4 oz. can cream of mushroom soup
10-oz. pkg. frozen green beans, thawed
1/2 c. chicken broth
2.8-oz. can French fried onions, divided
6 boneless, skinless chicken breasts
seasoned salt and pepper to taste

Shake flour in a large oven bag; arrange in a 13"x9" baking pan. Add soup, green beans, broth and half the onions to the bag. Sprinkle chicken with seasoned salt and pepper to taste. Arrange chicken in oven bag on top of soup mixture. Sprinkle remaining onions over chicken. Close bag with nylon tie provided; cut six, 1/2-inch slits in bag. Bake at 350 degrees for 45 to 50 minutes, until chicken juices run clear. Stir sauce in bag; spoon over chicken.

Heidi Maurer, *Garrett, IN*

Hunter's Pie

My 3-year-old son Hunter loves this and my 8-year-old son Luke does too...but without the beans!

Serves 4

1 lb. roast beef, cooked and cubed
12-oz. jar beef gravy
8-oz. can sliced carrots, drained
8-oz. can green beans, drained
9-inch deep-dish pie crust, baked
11-oz. tube refrigerated bread sticks

Combine all ingredients except pie crust and bread sticks; spread into pie crust. Arrange unbaked bread sticks on top, criss-cross style. Bake at 350 degrees for 20 minutes, or until heated through and bread sticks are golden.

Cheesy Baked Tortellini

Pat Wissler, *Harrisburg, PA*

Cheesy Baked Tortellini

When I make this hearty dish, I usually double the recipe and freeze some for later...very convenient!

Serves 4 to 6

10-oz. pkg. refrigerated cheese tortellini
2 c. marinara sauce
1/3 c. mascarpone cheese or softened cream cheese
1/4 c. fresh Italian parsley, chopped
2 t. fresh thyme, chopped
5 slices smoked mozzarella cheese
1/4 c. shredded Parmesan cheese

Prepare tortellini according to package directions; drain and set aside. Meanwhile, in a bowl, combine marinara sauce, mascarpone or cream cheese, parsley and thyme. Fold in tortellini. Transfer to a greased 9"x9" baking pan. Top with mozzarella and Parmesan cheeses. Bake, covered, at 350 degrees for about 30 minutes, or until cheese is melted and sauce is bubbly.

~ *Simple Swap* ~

Don't have a specialty cheese on hand for a recipe? Many recipes work well with a simple substitution. For example, provolone and Monterey Jack are great swaps for mozzarella.

Paula Purcell, *Plymouth Meeting, PA*

Easy Pork Chop-Potato Dinner

My mom used to serve this when my best friend, Chris, came to dinner. As we got older, Chris and I would make it ourselves...real comfort food!

Serves 8 to 10

1/2 c. oil
1/4 c. water
6 to 8 potatoes, sliced
2 onions, sliced
salt, pepper and garlic salt to taste
8 to 10 boneless pork chops
Optional: dry mustard

Pour oil and water into a 13"x9" baking pan sprayed with non-stick cooking spray. Layer potato and onion slices on bottom of pan; sprinkle to taste with salt, pepper and garlic salt. Arrange pork chops over vegetables. Sprinkle with additional salt, pepper, garlic salt and mustard, if desired. Cover tightly with aluminum foil and bake at 375 degrees for 45 minutes. Remove aluminum foil; bake for an additional 10 to 15 minutes, until tender and golden.

Tammy Rowe, *Bellevue, OH*

Rooster Pie

The aroma of country goodness fills the house as it's baking...we can hardly wait to break the golden crust!

Serves 4 to 6

2 c. cooked chicken, cubed
1/2 c. frozen carrots
1/2 c. frozen peas
1 onion, diced
3 T. pimentos, chopped
1 T. fresh parsley, chopped
salt and pepper to taste
10-3/4 oz. can cream of chicken soup
1 c. sour cream
1 c. chicken broth
11-1/2 oz. tube refrigerated biscuits

Combine chicken, carrots, peas, onion, pimentos, parsley, salt and pepper; set aside. Combine soup, sour cream and broth; stir into chicken mixture. Spread in a greased 13"x9" baking pan. Arrange biscuits over top. Bake at 350 degrees for 30 minutes, or until biscuits are golden.

Christi Wroe, *Bedford, PA*

Meatball Sub Casserole

Serve this tasty casserole with a green salad and garlic bread...delicious!

Serves 4

1 loaf Italian bread, cut into 1-inch thick slices
8-oz. pkg. cream cheese, softened
1/2 c. mayonnaise
1 t. Italian seasoning
1/4 t. pepper
2 c. shredded mozzarella cheese, divided
1-lb. pkg. frozen meatballs, thawed
28-oz. jar pasta sauce
1 c. water

Arrange bread slices in a single layer in an ungreased 13"x9" baking pan; set aside. In a bowl, combine cream cheese, mayonnaise and seasonings; spread over bread slices. Sprinkle with 1/2 cup cheese; set aside. Gently mix together meatballs, spaghetti sauce and water; spoon over cheese. Sprinkle with remaining cheese. Bake, uncovered, at 350 degrees for 30 minutes.

Flavor Booster

.... ✳ ....

For a tasty change in recipes, try substituting flavored cream cheese for plain. You'll be amazed at how much flavor you'll be adding!

Sausage & Chicken Cassoulet

Diane Stout, *Zeeland, MI*

Sausage & Chicken Cassoulet

This savory casserole is full of wonderful flavors... better bring along some recipe cards to share!

Serves 4 to 6

1 lb. hot Italian ground pork sausage
1 c. carrot, peeled and thinly sliced
1 onion, diced
2 t. garlic, minced
1 c. red wine or beef broth
2 T. tomato paste
1 bay leaf
1 t. dried thyme
1 t. dried rosemary
salt and pepper to taste
2 c. cooked chicken, diced
2 15-oz. cans Great Northern beans

Brown sausage in an oven-safe Dutch oven over medium heat; drain. Add carrot, onion and garlic. Sauté for 3 minutes. Add wine or broth, tomato paste and seasonings; bring to a boil. Remove from heat; stir in chicken and beans with liquid. Bake, covered, at 350 degrees for 45 minutes, or until bubbly. Discard bay leaf before serving.

Jenny Poole, *Salisbury, NC*

Turkey-Spinach Quiche

This recipe is a holiday tradition at our house. I bake it in muffin tins for a nice presentation...my guests love it.

Serves 4 to 6

1 lb. ground turkey sausage, browned and drained
3 c. shredded Cheddar cheese
10-oz. pkg. frozen chopped spinach, cooked
    and drained
8-oz. can sliced mushrooms, drained
2/3 c. onion, chopped
1 c. mayonnaise
1 c. milk
4 eggs, beaten
1-1/4 c. biscuit baking mix
2 T. cornstarch

Mix all ingredients together and pour into a greased 9" pie plate. Bake at 350 degrees for 35 to 40 minutes, until golden and set.

~ *Simple Swap* ~

No ground turkey on hand? Substitute ground chicken, beef or even ground pork!

Brenda Doak, *Delaware, OH*

Swiss Bliss

I've had this recipe over 30 years. It's great with mashed potatoes.

Serves 4 to 6

2 lbs. beef chuck roast, cut into 4 to 6 pieces
1-1/2 oz. pkg. onion soup mix
16-oz. can chopped tomatoes, drained and 1/2 c. juice
   reserved
8-oz. pkg. sliced mushrooms
1/2 green pepper, sliced
1/4 t. salt
pepper to taste
1 T. steak sauce
1 T. cornstarch
1 T. fresh parsley, chopped

Arrange beef pieces, slightly overlapping, on a greased 20-inch length of aluminum foil. Sprinkle with onion soup mix; top with tomatoes, mushrooms, green pepper, salt and pepper. Mix together reserved tomato juice, steak sauce and cornstarch; pour over beef and vegetables. Fold aluminum foil up over all and double-fold edges to seal tightly. Place foil package in a baking pan. Bake at 375 degrees for 2 hours, or until tender. Sprinkle with parsley.

Judi Leaming, *Dover, DE*

Baked Chicken Chow Mein

Our daughter, Ami, earned a 4-H Blue Ribbon for thi dish!

Serves 4 to 6

10-3/4 oz. can cream of chicken soup
10-3/4 oz. can cream of celery soup
5-oz. can evaporated milk
4-oz. can mushroom stems and pieces, drained
8-oz. can water chestnuts, drained and chopped
2 c. cooked chicken, cubed
5-oz. can chow mein noodles, divided
2 t. Worcestershire sauce
1 to 2 t. curry powder
2 T. butter

In a bowl, combine soups and milk; fold in mushrooms, water chestnuts, chicken and half the chow mein noodles. Sprinkle with Worcestershire sauce and curry powder; stir to combine. Spread into a greased 2-quart casserole dish. Top with remaining noodles; dot with butter. Bake, uncovered, at 350 degrees for 30 minutes, or until bubbly.

Baked Chicken Chow Mein

Special Spanish Pot Roast

Linda Newkirk, *Central Point, OR*

Special Spanish Pot Roast

A good friend shared this recipe with me years ago. I've prepared it many times for family and guests.

Serves 4 to 6

8-oz. bottle Catalina salad dressing, divided
3-lb. beef chuck roast
6 to 8 carrots, peeled and diced
6 to 8 potatoes, peeled and diced
Optional: 1 onion, quartered
12-oz. jar green olives with pimentos

Heat 1/4 cup dressing in a roasting pan over medium heat. Add roast to pan; cook and turn until all sides are browned. Add carrots, potatoes and onion, if using, to pan. Pour remaining dressing over all; top with olives and olive juice. Cover and bake at 350 degrees for 2 to 3 hours, to desired doneness.

Jeanne Berfiend, *Indianapolis, IN*

Saucy Chicken & Rice

Add a teaspoon of dried thyme for a savory touch.

Serves 6

10-3/4 oz. can cream of mushroom soup
10-3/4 oz. can cream of chicken soup
10-3/4 oz. can cream of celery soup
1-3/4 c. instant rice, uncooked
1-1/2 oz. pkg. onion soup mix

2 c. water
6 boneless, skinless chicken breasts

Combine all ingredients except chicken in a 13"x9" baking pan. Gently push chicken breasts into the mixture until they are partly covered. Cover pan; bake at 350 degrees for 1-1/2 hours. Uncover and bake an additional 30 minutes.

Vickie, *Gooseberry Patch*

Cheesy Turkey Rellenos

Try tossing in some jalapeños for a hotter version!

Serves 6

4 4-oz. cans whole green chiles, drained and rinsed
1/4 lb. Pepper Jack cheese, sliced into 1/2-inch strips
2 c. cooked turkey, sliced into 1/2-inch strips
1/2 c. all-purpose flour
1/2 t. baking powder
1/4 t. salt
1/2 c. milk
3 eggs, beaten
2/3 c. shredded Cheddar cheese

Slice chiles up one side; remove seeds and spread open flat. Arrange in a greased 11"x7" baking pan. Fill each chile half with Pepper Jack cheese and turkey strips. Fold chiles closed and place seam-side down in pan. In a medium bowl, combine flour, baking powder and salt. Whisk together milk and eggs; slowly add to flour mixture, beating until smooth. Pour over chiles. Bake at 450 degrees for 15 minutes. Remove from oven and turn off heat. Sprinkle Cheddar cheese over top and return to oven until cheese is melted.

Jenny Flake, *Gilbert, AZ*

Chicken Tex-Mex Bake

Simply stated...my family loves this dish!

Serves 8

2 12-1/2 oz. cans chicken, drained and shredded
2 10-oz. cans mild red enchilada sauce
10-3/4 oz. can cream of chicken soup
4-oz. can diced green chiles
14-1/2 oz. can diced tomatoes
2-1/2 c. shredded Mexican-blend cheese, divided
1 c. sour cream
1/2 c. onion, diced
1/2 t. pepper
10 flour tortillas, cut into 1-inch squares and divided
1/2 c. sliced black olives

Combine first 5 ingredients and half of the cheese; mix well. Blend in sour cream, onion and pepper; set aside. Arrange half the tortillas over the bottom of a 13"x9" baking pan sprayed with non-stick vegetable spray. Spoon a layer of chicken mixture over tortillas. Repeat layering, ending with chicken mixture on top. Sprinkle with remaining cheese; top with olives. Cover lightly with aluminum foil; bake at 350 degrees for 40 minutes, or until hot and bubbly.

Missy Pluta, *Portage, MI*

Puffy Potato Casserole

Scatter French fried onions on top for a crunchy garnish.

Serves 4 to 6

1 lb. ground beef, browned and drained
10-3/4 oz. can cream of mushroom soup
10-3/4 oz. can cream of chicken soup
2 14-1/2 oz. cans green beans, drained
8 slices American cheese
32-oz. pkg. frozen potato puffs

Spoon ground beef into a 13"x9" baking pan; top with soups. Layer green beans over soups; arrange cheese slices on top. Top with a single layer of potato puffs. Bake at 350 degrees for 30 to 40 minutes.

Flavor Booster
.... ✳ ....

Serve up authentic Mexican fruits & vegetables alongside dinner...jícamas, papayas, avocados and mangoes are all easy to find at the local grocery.

Puffy Potato Casserole

Country Chicken Pot Pie

Kris Coburn, *Dansville, NY*

Country Chicken Pot Pie

Just like Mom used to make! It's a delicious way to use up leftover chicken and cooked vegetables too.

Serves 4 to 6

2 9-inch pie crusts, divided
1-1/2 c. cooked chicken, diced
2 to 3 c. frozen mixed vegetables, thawed
2 10-3/4 oz. cans cream of chicken soup
1/2 c. milk
1 t. pepper
1 t. dried thyme
1 egg, beaten

Line a 9" pie plate with one crust. Mix together chicken, vegetables, soup, milk, pepper and thyme; spread in crust. Top with remaining crust; cut slits to vent and brush with egg. Bake at 350 degrees for 50 minutes,

Cook it Quick

All out of cream of chicken soup? Try using cream of mushroom or cream of celery soup instead.

Kim Turechek, *Oklahoma City, OK*

Sour Cream-Chicken Enchiladas

Keep extra sour cream, salsa, green onions and shredded cheese on hand for topping off each serving.

Makes 12 servings

2 10-3/4 oz. cans cream of chicken soup
4-oz. can diced green chiles, drained
1/2 c. milk
1/2 t. ground cumin
1 c. sour cream
2 c. cooked chicken, cubed
3-oz. pkg. cream cheese, softened
1/4 c. onion, chopped
12 10-inch flour tortillas
1 c. shredded Monterey Jack cheese

Combine the first 5 ingredients in a blender; blend until smooth. Set aside. Mix chicken, cream cheese and onion together; spread one to 2 tablespoons chicken mixture onto each tortilla. Roll up; place seam-side down in an ungreased 13"x9" baking pan. Top with soup mixture; sprinkle with cheese. Cover; bake at 350 degrees for 30 minutes. Uncover the last 5 minutes of baking.

Audrey Lett, *Newark, DE*

Turkey & Pasta Bake

No one will complain about leftover turkey when you prepare this casserole. Always a winner!

Serves 6

6 c. cooked penne pasta
2 c. cooked turkey, cubed
2 c. plum tomatoes, coarsely chopped and drained
8-oz. container cottage cheese
1/2 c. shredded Cheddar cheese
4 green onions, sliced
1 t. dried basil
1/2 t. dried oregano
1/3 c. dry bread crumbs
2 T. dried parsley

Combine pasta, turkey and tomatoes. Spread in a greased 13"x9" baking pan; set aside. In a small bowl, combine cottage cheese, Cheddar cheese, onions, basil and oregano. Mix well. Spread over turkey mixture, smoothing with the back of the spoon. Toss bread crumbs with parsley and sprinkle over top. Bake at 350 degrees for 30 minutes.

Flavor Booster

Shake up a recipe for a change of pace. Use fettuccine or angel hair pasta in main dishes or try rotini or wagon wheel pasta in salads.

Carrie Knotts, *Kalispell, MT*

Spicy Sausage & Chicken Creole

I used this dish to win over my husband and his fami while we were dating. He likes his food spicy! Of course, you can use a little less hot pepper sauce if you prefer.

Serves 4

14-1/2 oz. can chopped tomatoes
1/2 c. long-cooking rice, uncooked
1/2 c. hot water
2 t. hot pepper sauce
1/4 t. garlic powder
1/4 t. dried oregano
16-oz. pkg. frozen broccoli, corn & red pepper blend, thawed
4 boneless, skinless chicken thighs
1/2 lb. link Italian pork sausage, cooked and quartere
8-oz. can tomato sauce

Combine tomatoes, rice, water, hot sauce and seasoning in a 13"x9" baking pan. Cover and bake at 375 degrees for 10 minutes. Stir vegetables into tomato mixture; top wi chicken and sausage. Pour tomato sauce over top. Bake, covered, at 375 degrees for 40 minutes, or until juices of chicken run clear.

Spicy Sausage & Chicken Creole

Oh-So-Easy Chicken & Veggies

Laura Fuller, Fort Wayne, IN

Oh-So-Easy Chicken & Veggies

Try this recipe with 3 turkey thighs, sweet potatoes and a bit of dried sage too.

Serves 4 to 6

2 T. all-purpose flour
2.6-oz. pkg. golden onion soup mix
1 c. water
3 carrots, peeled and diced
2 redskin potatoes, cut in wedges
1 green pepper, cubed
6 boneless, skinless chicken breasts
seasoned salt to taste
pepper to taste

Shake flour in a large oven bag; arrange bag in a 13"x9" baking pan. Add soup mix and water to bag; squeeze bag to blend flour. Add carrots, potatoes and green pepper; turn bag to coat ingredients. Sprinkle chicken with seasoned salt and pepper to taste; arrange in bag on top of vegetables. Close bag with nylon tie provided; cut six, 1/2-inch slits in top. Tuck ends of bag into pan. Bake at 350 degrees for 55 to 60 minutes, until chicken is tender and juices run clear.

Jennie Gist, Gooseberry Patch

Crab & Shrimp Casserole

The great taste of the sea in a convenient casserole!

Serves 4 to 6

2 8-oz. cans crabmeat, drained
2 4-oz. cans tiny shrimp, drained
2 c. celery, chopped
1 green pepper, chopped
1 onion, chopped
1 T. Worcestershire sauce
1 t. sugar
1 c. mayonnaise
salt and pepper to taste
1 c. soft bread crumbs, buttered
2 T. lemon juice
Garnish: thin lemon slices

Mix together all ingredients except bread crumbs, lemon juice and garnish. Place in a greased 13"x9" baking pan. Spread bread crumbs over crab mixture. Bake, uncovered, at 350 degrees for 30 to 45 minutes, until heated through. Sprinkle lemon juice over casserole. Garnish with lemon slices.

Katie French, Portland, TX

Velvet Chicken

When I got married, my sister made a book of family recipes for me. This particular recipe was my sister-in-law's contribution to the book, and it is great.

Serves 6 to 8

6 to 8 boneless, skinless chicken breasts, cooked and cubed
10-3/4 oz. can cream of chicken soup
8-oz. container sour cream
1/2 c. margarine, melted
8-oz. pkg. pasteurized processed cheese spread, shredded
1 sleeve buttery round crackers, crushed

Combine chicken, soup and sour cream. Spread in a greased 13"x9" baking pan. Pour melted margarine over top; sprinkle with shredded cheese, then crushed crackers. Bake at 350 degrees for 20 minutes.

Jo Ann, *Gooseberry Patch*

Reuben Casserole

An all-time favorite deli sandwich turned into a quick and simple casserole!

Serves 6

6 slices rye bread, cubed
16-oz. can sauerkraut, drained and rinsed
1 lb. sliced deli corned beef, cut into strips
3/4 c. Thousand Island salad dressing
2 c. shredded Swiss cheese

Arrange bread cubes in a greased 13"x9" baking pan; cover with sauerkraut. Layer corned beef over sauerkraut; drizzle salad dressing over top. Cover with aluminum foil and bake at 400 degrees for 20 minutes. Remove foil; sprinkle with cheese and bake, uncovered, for another 10 minutes, or until cheese is melted and bubbly.

Cathy Rutz, *Andover, KS*

Simple Turkey Pot Pie

Topped with buttermilk biscuits, this pot pie is surprisingly simple to prepare, yet every bit as tasty as you'd expect.

Serves 6

16-oz. pkg. frozen mixed vegetables, thawed and drained
2 14-3/4 oz. cans creamed corn
10-3/4 oz. can cream of mushroom soup
3/4 c. milk
2 c. cooked turkey, chopped
2 12-oz. tubes refrigerated buttermilk biscuits, quartered

Mix vegetables, corn, soup, milk and turkey; pour into a 13"x9" baking pan sprayed with non-stick vegetable spray. Top with biscuits; bake at 350 degrees for 35 to 40 minutes, until biscuits are golden.

Kerry Mayer, *Dunham Springs, LA*

Western Pork Chops

For a delicious variation, try substituting peeled, cubed sweet potatoes for the redskins.

Serves 4

1 T. all-purpose flour
1 c. barbecue sauce
4 pork chops
salt and pepper to taste
4 redskin potatoes, sliced
1 green pepper, cubed
1 c. baby carrots

Shake flour in a large oven bag; place in a 13"x9" baking pan. Add barbecue sauce to oven bag; squeeze bag to blend in flour. Season pork chops with salt and pepper; add pork chops and vegetables to oven bag. Turn bag to coat ingredients with sauce; arrange vegetables in an even layer with pork chops on top. Close bag with nylon tie provided; cut six, 1/2-inch slits in top. Bake at 350 degrees for about 40 to 45 minutes, until pork chops and vegetables are tender.

Western Pork Chops

South-of-the-Border Chicken

Penny Sherman, *Cumming, GA*

South-of-the-Border Chicken

Scrumptious...makes any meal a fiesta!

Serves 4

2 T. all-purpose flour
14-1/2 oz. can diced tomatoes with chili seasoning
2 t. diced jalapeños
1/2 t. salt
15-oz. can black beans, drained and rinsed
6 boneless, skinless chicken breasts
1 yellow pepper, sliced

Shake flour in a large oven bag; place bag in a 13"x9" baking pan. Add tomatoes, jalapeños and salt to bag; squeeze to blend with flour. Add beans and chicken to bag; turn to coat chicken. Top with yellow pepper. Close bag with nylon tie provided; cut six, 1/2-inch slits in top. Bake at 350 degrees for 45 to 50 minutes, until chicken juices run clear.

Theresa Currie, *Chatham, NJ*

Veggie-Chicken Bake

A quick-to-fix dish that's rich & creamy.

Serves 6 to 8

4 boneless, skinless chicken breasts, cooked and diced
1 c. mayonnaise
1 c. shredded Cheddar cheese
2 10-3/4 oz. cans cream of chicken soup
16-oz. pkg. frozen broccoli and cauliflower, thawed and drained
12-oz. pkg. egg noodles, cooked

Combine chicken, mayonnaise, cheese, soup and vegetables. Spoon into an ungreased 13"x9" baking pan; bake, uncovered, at 350 degrees, or until heated through. Serve over cooked noodles.

~ *Cook it Quick* ~

An oh-so-easy way to cook up egg noodles: when water comes to a rolling boil, turn off the heat. Add the noodles and cover the pot. Let stand for 20 minutes, stirring once or twice...done!

Amy Butcher, *Columbus, GA*

Southwestern Turkey Casserole

I like to arrange bowls filled with different toppings so everyone can garnish with their favorites...sour cream, chopped cilantro, salsa, chopped green onions and extra shredded cheese.

Makes 6 to 8 servings

10-3/4 oz. can cream of chicken soup
10-3/4 oz. can cream of mushroom soup
7-oz. can diced green chiles, drained
1 c. sour cream
16 6-inch corn tortillas, cut into strips
2 c. cooked turkey, diced and divided
8-oz. pkg. shredded Cheddar cheese, divided

Combine soups, chiles and sour cream in a mixing bowl; set aside. Line the bottom of a 13"x9" baking pan with half the tortilla strips. Top with half the turkey. Spread half the soup mixture over turkey; sprinkle with half the cheese. Repeat layers. Bake at 350 degrees for 30 to 45 minutes.

Shirley Gist, *Zanesville, OH*

Turkey Tetrazzini

Gobbles up leftovers...a must for the day after Thanksgiving!

Makes 6 servings

8-oz. pkg. thin spaghetti, uncooked
2 cubes chicken bouillon
2 to 3 T. dried, minced onion
2 10-3/4 oz. cans cream of mushroom soup
8-oz. container sour cream
1/2 c. milk
salt and pepper to taste
2 c. cooked turkey, cubed
8-oz. can sliced mushrooms, drained
8-oz. pkg. shredded Cheddar cheese

Cook spaghetti according to package directions, adding bouillon and onion to cooking water. Drain and place in a large bowl. Stir together soup, sour cream, milk, salt and pepper in a medium bowl; fold in turkey and mushrooms. Lightly stir mixture into spaghetti, coating well. Pour into a lightly greased 13"x9" baking pan; top with cheese. Bake at 350 degrees for 30 to 40 minutes, until hot and bubbly.

Turkey Tetrazzini

Balsamic Rosemary Chicken

Bobbi-Jo Thornton, *Hancock, ME*

Balsamic Rosemary Chicken

The zing of balsamic vinegar really adds flavor.

Makes 4 servings

4 boneless, skinless chicken breasts
2 T. Dijon mustard
salt and pepper to taste
2 T. garlic, minced
2 T. water
1/4 c. balsamic vinegar
4 sprigs fresh rosemary

Arrange chicken in an ungreased 11"x7" baking pan. Spread mustard over chicken; sprinkle with salt, pepper and garlic. Blend water and vinegar; sprinkle over chicken. Arrange one sprig of rosemary on each chicken breast; cover with aluminum foil and refrigerate for 2 to 3 hours. Bake, covered, at 350 degrees for 20 minutes; uncover and bake for an additional 10 minutes, or until chicken is golden. Discard rosemary before serving.

> ⁓ *Handy Tip* ⁓
> Create a personal herb garden! Choose a narrow wooden crate that will fit on a windowsill. Fill it with starter pots of herbs...rosemary, basil, oregano and thyme make a yummy kitchen sampler.

Jen Licon-Conner, *Gooseberry Patch*

Anytime Enchurritos

This recipe is a natural alongside refried beans and corn cakes.

Makes 6 to 8 servings

2 c. turkey, cooked and shredded
1-1/2 c. salsa, divided
1 c. sour cream
2 to 3 T. diced green chiles
8 10-inch flour tortillas
10-3/4 oz. can cream of chicken soup
2 c. shredded Mexican-blend cheese

Combine turkey, 1/2 cup salsa, sour cream and chiles. Spoon turkey mixture into tortillas; roll up and place seam-side down in an ungreased 13"x9" baking pan. Blend together soup and remaining salsa; pour over tortillas. Bake, uncovered, at 350 degrees for 30 minutes. Sprinkle with cheese and bake an additional 5 minutes, or until cheese is melted.

Holly Sutton, *Middleburgh, NY*

Stuffed Pasta Shells

You'll have just enough time to make a crispy salad while this casserole is baking...it's ready in just 30 minutes.

Makes 6 to 8 servings

1-1/2 c. chicken-flavored stuffing mix, prepared
2 c. cooked chicken, chopped
1/2 c. peas
1/2 c. mayonnaise
18 jumbo pasta shells, cooked
10-3/4 oz. can cream of chicken soup
2/3 c. water

Combine stuffing, chicken, peas and mayonnaise; spoon into cooked pasta shells. Arrange shells in a greased 13"x9" baking pan. Mix soup and water; pour over shells. Cover and bake at 350 degrees for 30 minutes.

Jen Stout, *Blandon, PA*

Sweet & Smoky Chicken

This is an old Pennsylvania Dutch recipe sure to please dinner guests.

Serves 6 to 8

3 lbs. chicken
1 onion, sliced
1/2 c. catsup
1/2 c. molasses
1/4 c. vinegar

1 t. smoke-flavored cooking sauce
1/4 t. pepper

Arrange chicken pieces in a greased 13"x9" baking pan; set aside. Stir together remaining ingredients; pour over chicken. Bake, uncovered, at 350 degrees for one hour, or until chicken juices run clear.

Lisa Hains, *Tipp City, OH*

Grecian Chicken

I like to put this in the oven before leaving for church.

Serves 8

8 boneless, skinless chicken breasts
8 to 10 potatoes, peeled and halved
8 to 10 carrots, peeled
2 T. dried rosemary
3 T. olive oil
3 T. lemon juice
salt and pepper to taste
1 t. garlic powder

Place chicken in a greased roasting pan; bake at 450 degrees until golden, about 20 minutes. Add potatoes and carrots to pan; pour in enough water to partially cover vegetables. Sprinkle with rosemary; drizzle with oil and lemon juice. Sprinkle with salt, pepper and garlic powder. Reduce oven to 350 degrees and bake, covered, about 3 hours, until vegetables are tender.

~ *Cook it Quick* ~

Spray the measuring cup with non-stick vegetable spray before measuring honey, molasses or peanut butter...the sticky stuff will slip right out!

Stuffed Pasta Shells

Cheesy Chicken & Mac

Myra Barker, *Gap, PA*

Cheesy Chicken & Mac

Having company? This overnight dish can be popped in the oven right before guests arrive.

Serves 6 to 8

2 c. cooked chicken, diced
2 c. elbow macaroni, uncooked
2 c. milk
2 10-3/4 oz. cans cream of mushroom soup
2 onions, diced
8-oz. pkg. pasteurized processed cheese spread, diced

Mix all ingredients together; spoon into an ungreased 13"x9" baking pan. Refrigerate overnight; bake at 350 degrees for one hour.

Flavor Booster
.... ✳ ....
**Fresh out of water chestnuts?
Try swapping in a jar of baby
corn for crunch and flavor.**

Beverly Stergeos, *Mansfield, TX*

Thankful Turkey Casserole

My mom's favorite day-after-Thanksgiving casserole, made with whatever roast turkey was left over. My family always looks forward to this special dish...yum!

Serves 6 to 8

2 c. cooked turkey or chicken, cubed
1/2 c. onion, chopped
1/4 c. celery, chopped
2-oz. pkg. slivered almonds
8-oz. can water chestnuts, drained and chopped
10-3/4 oz. can cream of chicken soup
1 c. mayonnaise
Garnish: 1 c. round buttery crackers, crushed
    cooked rice or egg noodles

Mix all ingredients except crackers and rice or noodles. Place in a lightly greased 2-quart casserole dish; top with crushed crackers. Bake, uncovered, at 350 degrees for about 20 minutes, until hot and bubbly. Serve over cooked rice or noodles.

Cabbage Roll Casserole

Dianne Gregory, *Sheridan, AR*

Cabbage Roll Casserole

The flavors of a tasty favorite without all the fuss!

Makes 10 to 12 servings

2 lbs. ground beef, browned
1 c. onion, chopped
29-oz. can tomato sauce
1 head cabbage, chopped
1 c. instant rice, uncooked
1 t. salt
14-oz. can beef broth

Combine all ingredients except broth in an ungreased, deep 13"x9" baking pan. Drizzle with broth; cover with aluminum foil. Bake at 350 degrees for one hour; uncover and stir. Cover again; bake 30 additional minutes, or until rice is cooked and casserole is heated through.

Flavor Booster

∙∙∙∙∙∙∙∙∙∙∙∙∙∙∙ ✳ ∙∙∙∙∙∙∙∙∙∙∙∙∙∙∙

**A dash of cider vinegar adds
zing to any cabbage dish!**

Pam Messner, *Gibbon, MN*

Oniony Zucchini Bake

When the zucchini is bursting in my garden, this is the recipe I turn to. It just can't be beat for taste.

Serves 6 to 8

3 c. zucchini, thinly sliced
4 eggs, beaten
1 c. biscuit baking mix
1/2 c. oil
1/2 c. onion, chopped
1/2 c. grated Parmesan cheese
2 T. fresh parsley, chopped
1/2 t. seasoned salt
1/2 t. dried oregano
1/2 t. salt
1/4 t. pepper

Mix all ingredients together. Pour into a greased 13"x9" baking pan. Bake at 350 degrees for 30 minutes.

Chapter Four

Stovetop Suppers

Easy stovetop meals are delicious and save time! When you need a quick dinner and don't want to bother with the oven, grab your favorite skillet or Dutch oven and get ready to wow your tastebuds with these tasty recipes. Orange-Pork Stir-Fry, Rigatoni with Blue Cheese and Skillet Macaroni & Beef are just a few of our favorites!

Liz Plotnick-Snay, *Gooseberry Patch*

My Favorite One-Pot Meal

Curry powder, raisins and chopped apple make this chicken dish just a little different.

Makes 3 to 4 servings

2 onions, diced
1/4 c. oil, divided
2-1/2 to 3 lbs. boneless, skinless chicken breasts
14-1/2 oz. can diced tomatoes
1/2 c. white wine or chicken broth
1 T. curry powder
1/4 t. garlic powder
1/4 t. dried thyme
1/4 t. nutmeg
1 apple, peeled, cored and cubed
1/4 c. raisins
3 T. whipping cream
1/2 t. lemon juice
2 c. cooked rice

Sauté onions in 2 tablespoons oil over medium heat in a large skillet; remove onions and set aside. Add remaining oil and chicken to skillet; cook chicken until golden. Return onions to skillet; add tomatoes with juice, wine or broth and spices. Mix well; reduce heat, cover and simmer for 20 minutes. Add apple, raisins and cream; simmer over low heat for an additional 6 to 8 minutes. Stir in lemon juice. Serve over cooked rice.

Peggy Sanders, *Adair, IA*

Taco in a Pan

This recipe was originally given to me by my mother. It's a family favorite that's asked for time & time again. I have since passed it on to my sons.

Serves 4 to 6

1 lb. ground beef
1/2 c. onion, chopped
1/2 c. green pepper, chopped
2 c. water
1-1/4 oz. pkg. taco seasoning mix
1-1/2 c. instant rice, uncooked
1 c. salsa, or to taste
1 c. shredded Colby Jack cheese
1 tomato, chopped
Optional: 1 c. sliced black olives
Garnish: crushed nacho-flavored tortilla chips

Brown beef, onion and green pepper in a skillet over medium heat; drain. Stir water and taco seasoning into beef mixture. Bring to a boil; stir in rice. Cover and cook for 3 to 5 minutes, until rice is tender. Sprinkle salsa and cheese over all. Remove from heat; cover and let stand until cheese melts. Top with tomato and olives, if desired. Garnish with chips.

Taco in a Pan

Bowties, Sausage & Beans

Amy Butcher, *Columbus, GA*

Orange-Pork Stir-Fry

Short on time? Pick up a package of pork that's precut in strips for stir-frying.

Makes 4 servings

1-oz. pkg. Italian salad dressing mix
1/4 c. orange juice
1/4 c. oil
2 T. soy sauce
1 lb. pork loin, cut into strips
16-oz. pkg. frozen Oriental vegetable blend, thawed
2-1/2 c. cooked rice

Mix together dressing mix, juice, oil and soy sauce. Combine one tablespoon of dressing mixture and pork strips in a large skillet over medium heat. Cook and stir for 4 to 5 minutes, until pork is no longer pink. Add vegetables and remaining dressing mixture; cook and stir until vegetables are crisp-tender. Serve over cooked rice.

Christy Young, *North Attleboro, MA*

Bowties, Sausage & Beans

This is a hearty and delicious meal anytime...stellar served with a side salad and thick slices of Italian bread.

Serves 6

1 T. olive oil
6 hot Italian pork sausage links, sliced into thirds
1 tomato, chopped
2 15-oz. cans cannellini beans
10-oz. pkg. fresh spinach
garlic powder and dried basil to taste
12-oz. pkg. bowtie pasta, cooked

Heat oil in a Dutch oven over medium heat. Cook sausage until browned on all sides and no longer pink in the center; stir in tomato. Simmer, stirring occasionally, until tomato is soft. Stir in beans and seasonings; heat through. Fold in spinach. Cover and simmer until spinach is wilted, about 6 to 8 minutes. Stir in pasta; toss to mix and heat through.

Glenna Martin, *Uwchland, PA*

Chicken Spaghetti

An old family favorite!

Serves 4

1 lb. boneless, skinless chicken breasts, cut into
   bite-size pieces
1/4 to 1/2 c. butter
1 onion, chopped
8-oz. can sliced mushrooms, drained
16-oz. pkg. broccoli flowerets
1 clove garlic, minced
salt and pepper to taste
16-oz. pkg. spaghetti, cooked
Garnish: grated Parmesan cheese

In a large skillet, sauté chicken in butter until no longer pink. Add onion, mushrooms, broccoli and garlic; sauté until chicken is cooked through and vegetables are tender. Add salt and pepper to taste; toss with cooked spaghetti. Sprinkle with Parmesan cheese.

Emma Brown, *Ontario, Canada*

Southwestern Corn Skillet

This is one of the easiest dishes I make. All the hearty southwestern flavors and gooey cheese...definitely a stick-to-your-ribs meal.

Serve 6

1 lb. ground beef
1/2 c. onion, chopped
26-oz. jar pasta sauce
11-oz. can sweet corn & diced peppers, drained
1/2 t. salt
8-oz. pkg rotini pasta, cooked
1 c. shredded Cheddar cheese
4 green onions, sliced

Brown beef and onion in a skillet over medium heat; drain. Stir in pasta sauce, corn, salt and pasta. Cook and stir until heated through. Remove from heat and sprinkle with cheese. Cover and let stand until cheese is melted; sprinkle with green onions.

Karen Jones, *Lebanon, OH*

Farmers' Dinner

A simple down-home dish to satisfy hearty appetites.

Serves 4 to 6

1 lb. bacon, cut in 2-inch pieces
2 14-1/2 oz. cans green beans, drained
15-1/4 oz. can corn, drained
6 potatoes, peeled and cubed
1-1/4 t. celery salt
1/2 t. salt
1/4 t. pepper

Cook bacon in a large stockpot over medium heat until tender, but not crisp. Drain half of drippings; add remaining ingredients. Mix well; cover and simmer for 2-1/2 to 3 hours.

Susan Dudley, *Austin, TX*

Chinese Beef & Noodles

I like to use a vegetable blend of broccoli, red peppers and water chestnuts for color.

Serves 4 to 6

1-1/4 lbs. ground beef
2 3-oz. pkgs. Oriental-flavored ramen noodles, crushed
2 c. frozen stir-fry vegetable blend, thawed
2 c. water
2 T. green onion, sliced

Brown ground beef in a skillet; drain. Stir in one seasoning packet; remove beef from skillet. Combine noodles, remaining seasoning packet, vegetables and water in skillet. Bring to a boil; reduce heat to medium. Cover and simmer for 3 minutes, or until noodles are tender, stirring occasionally. Return browned beef to skillet; heat through. Stir in green onion and mix well.

─ *Handy Tip* ─
A range of cooking times is often given on packages of pasta. The first cooking time is for al dente (firm to the bite) and the second cooking time is for a softer pasta. You choose!

Lou Miller, *Savannah, MO*

Skillet Macaroni & Beef

This is my favorite recipe...I usually have all the ingredients on hand and my guests always love its hearty flavor.

Serves 6 to 8

1-1/2 lbs. ground beef
2 c. elbow macaroni, uncooked
1/2 c. onion, minced
1/2 c. green pepper, chopped
2 8-oz. cans tomato sauce
1 c. water
1 T. Worcestershire sauce
1 t. salt
1/4 t. pepper

Lightly brown beef in a skillet; drain. Stir in macaroni, onion and green pepper; heat until onion is soft. Add remaining ingredients. Lower heat; cover and simmer 25 minutes, or until macaroni is tender, stirring occasionally.

Southwestern Corn Skillet

Beef Porcupine Meatballs

Terri Lock, *Carrollton, MO*

Beef Porcupine Meatballs

As a teacher, I need fast homestyle meals to serve to my family of five before I leave for evening school events...this recipe is perfect.

ermicelli mix

nicelli mix, beef and egg,
from mix. Form mixture
illet over medium heat, cook
nally, until browned on all
bine seasoning packet and
ls. Cover and simmer for
kened and meatballs are no
r. Serve meatballs and sauce

vor Booster

·············· ✳ ··················

Jazz up an ordinary dinner with
something new...chile peppers,
spicy salsa, water chestnuts or
baby corn.

Mandi Smith, *Delaware, OH*

Salsa Ranch Skillet

I created this delicious recipe for competition in the Ohio State Fair. It's very tasty, quick and easy to make.

Serves 4 to 6

1 lb. ground beef
1/2 c. sweet onion, chopped
1/2 c. green pepper, chopped
2.8-oz. pkg. ranch salad dressing mix
1 c. water
15-oz. can tomato sauce
16-oz. jar mild salsa
16-oz. can baked beans
8-oz. pkg. rotini pasta, uncooked
1 c. shredded Colby & Monterey Jack cheese

Brown ground beef with onion and green pepper in a large skillet over high heat. Stir in dressing mix until thoroughly blended. Stir in water, tomato sauce, salsa and beans; bring to a boil. Add pasta; reduce to medium-low heat. Simmer for 12 to 15 minutes, until pasta is tender, stirring occasionally. Remove from heat; sprinkle with cheese and let stand for 5 minutes until cheese melts and sauce thickens.

Sarah Jose, *Shreveport, LA*

One-Pot Beef Ravioli

This recipe is the perfect solution for a busy weeknight. I can have this on the table in less than 30 minutes, and there's only one pot to wash!

Serves 4

1 lb. lean ground beef
1 t. oil
1 onion, diced
8-oz. pkg. sliced mushrooms
2 cloves garlic, minced
2 26-oz. jars tomato-basil pasta sauce
1 c. water
1 T. Italian seasoning
1/2 t. salt
1/4 t. pepper
20-oz. pkg. refrigerated 4-cheese ravioli
1 c. shredded mozzarella cheese

Brown beef in a Dutch oven over medium-high heat; drain and set beef aside in a bowl. Add oil to Dutch oven; sauté onion and mushrooms for 8 minutes, or until tender. Add garlic and cook for one minute. Stir in beef, pasta sauce, water and seasonings; bring to a boil. Add ravioli to sauce; reduce heat to medium-low. Cover and simmer, stirring occasionally, for 8 to 10 minutes, until pasta is cooked. Stir in cheese.

Tanya Schroeder, *Cincinnati, OH*

Low-Country Shrimp Boil

This meal is so much fun...how often do you get to eat your whole meal with your hands? Kids love it, adults love it, and it's a great summer party idea!

Serves 6 to 8

6 qts. water
3/4 c. seafood seasoning
2 lbs. new redskin potatoes
2 lbs. smoked pork sausage, cut into 1-inch pieces
5 ears corn, husked and halved
2 lbs. uncooked large shrimp, cleaned
Garnish: cocktail sauce, melted butter, lemon wedges

Combine water and seasoning in a large pot; bring to a boil. Add potatoes and boil, covered, for 15 minutes. Add sausage and continue to boil for 5 minutes. Add corn; boil for another 5 minutes. Add shrimp and boil until shrimp are pink, about 4 minutes. Drain and transfer mixture to a large serving bowl. Garnish as desired.

Flavor Booster

················· ✻ ·················

A snappy seafood sauce! Just use measurements to suit your taste. Add lemon juice, lemon zest and capers to a mixture of mayonnaise and sour cream. Sprinkle with a dash of salt & pepper.

One-Pot Beef Ravioli

Farmhouse Pork & Cabbage Sauté

I wanted to try something different from the usual cabbage rolls, so I whipped up this tasty recipe. What an amazing blend of flavors...it's now one of my family's favorites!

Makes 4 servings

4 pork loin chops
1/4 t. salt
1/8 t. pepper
6 slices bacon, crisply cooked, crumbled and
   drippings reserved
1 t. olive oil
1 onion, thinly sliced
16-oz. pkg. shredded coleslaw mix
2 Golden Delicious apples, cored and sliced
3/4 lb. redskin potatoes, cubed
3/4 c. apple cider
1/4 t. dried thyme
1 T. cider vinegar

Season pork with salt and pepper; set aside. Heat reserved bacon drippings and oil in a Dutch oven over medium-high heat. Cook pork until golden on both sides, about 8 minutes. Remove pork and keep warm. Add onion to pan. Cover and cook over medium heat for 8 to 10 minutes, stirring occasionally, until golden. Gradually stir in coleslaw; cook until wilted, about 5 minutes. Add remaining ingredients except vinegar; bring to a boil. Reduce heat; cover and simmer for 15 minutes, or until potatoes are tender. Stir in vinegar; return pork to pan and heat through. Sprinkle with reserved bacon.

Karen Pilcher, *Burleson, TX*

Crunchy Crab Dish

A light and tasty dish with a double crunch of almonds and chow mein noodles.

Serves 6

3 T. butter
1 lb. crabmeat
8-3/4 oz. can crushed pineapple, drained and
   juice reserved
1/2 c. celery, sliced
2 T. cornstarch
2 c. chicken broth
1/2 c. slivered almonds, toasted
1 T. lemon juice
5-oz. can chow mein noodles

Melt butter in a skillet; add crabmeat, pineapple and celery. Cook over low heat for 5 minutes, stirring frequently. Set aside. Dissolve cornstarch in reserved juice; stir into crab mixture. Gradually pour in broth; simmer until thick. Mix in almonds and lemon juice; serve over chow mein noodles.

Lauren Kelly, *Wakefield, MA*

Chicken à la Audrey

If your grocery store doesn't carry the bellflower-shaped campanelle pasta, just substitute rotini or penne pasta.

Serves 4

2 to 3 T. olive oil
4 boneless, skinless chicken breasts, cut into
　bite-size pieces
1 red onion, sliced
1 green pepper, sliced
1 red pepper, sliced
1 clove garlic, minced
salt and pepper to taste
3/4 c. chicken broth
1/8 t. lemon juice
1/4 c. white wine or chicken broth
8-oz. pkg. cream cheese, softened
1 t. spicy mustard
8-oz. pkg. campanelle pasta, cooked

Heat oil in a skillet; add chicken and onion. Cook and stir until chicken is no longer pink; stir in peppers and garlic. Cook for 4 minutes; sprinkle with salt and pepper to taste. Add chicken broth, lemon juice and wine or additional broth; reduce heat to medium. Bring to a boil; add cream cheese and mustard. Stir well; reduce heat, cover and simmer for about 10 minutes. Stir in cooked pasta.

Kari Hodges, *Jacksonville, TX*

Skillet Goulash

I like to serve up this old-fashioned family favorite with thick slices of freshly baked sweet cornbread topped with pats of butter.

Makes 8 to 10 servings

2 lbs. ground beef
10-oz. can diced tomatoes with green chiles
6 baking potatoes, peeled and diced
15-oz. can tomato sauce
15-1/4 oz. can corn, drained
14-1/2 oz. can ranch-style beans
salt and pepper to taste

Brown beef in a Dutch oven over medium heat; drain. Add tomatoes with juice and remaining ingredients; reduce heat. Cover and simmer until potatoes are tender and mixture has thickened, about 45 minutes.

Trisha Donley, *Pinedale, WY*

Skillet Bowtie Lasagna

This is one of my favorite go-to meals. I love to serve it with a fresh green salad and slices of warm, buttered Italian bread.

Serves 4

1 lb. ground beef
1 onion, chopped
1 clove garlic, chopped
14-1/2 oz. can diced tomatoes
1-1/2 c. water
6-oz. can tomato paste
1 T. dried parsley
2 t. dried oregano
1 t. salt
2-1/2 c. bowtie pasta, uncooked
3/4 c. small-curd cottage cheese
1/4 c. grated Parmesan cheese

In a large skillet over medium heat, brown beef, onion and garlic; drain. Add tomatoes with juice, water, tomato paste and seasonings; mix well. Stir in pasta; bring to a boil. Reduce heat, cover and simmer for 20 to 25 minutes, until pasta is tender, stirring once. Combine cheeses; drop by rounded tablespoonfuls onto pasta mixture. Cover and cook for 5 minutes.

Zoe Bennett, *Columbia, SC*

Rigatoni with Blue Cheese

Feel free to substitute your favorite tube pasta like penne or mostaccioli.

Serves 4 to 6

16-oz. pkg. rigatoni pasta, uncooked
2 T. butter
1/2 c. crumbled blue cheese
2 T. grated Parmesan cheese
pepper to taste

Cook rigatoni according to package directions; drain and return to pot. Add butter and cheeses; stir to mix until melted. Sprinkle with pepper to taste.

Marian Buckley, *Fontana, CA*

Cheesy Rotini & Broccoli

Replace the broccoli with asparagus tips for variety.

Serves 4

1-1/2 c. rotini pasta, uncooked
2 carrots, peeled and sliced
1 c. broccoli flowerets
10-3/4 oz. can Cheddar cheese soup
1/2 c. milk
1/2 c. shredded Cheddar cheese
1 T. mustard

Cook pasta according to package directions. Add carrots and broccoli during last 5 minutes of cooking time; drain and return to pot. Pour soup, milk, cheese and mustard into pasta mixture; heat through.

Connie Seago, *Sinton, TX*

Chicken-Rice Skillet

This was one of my mother's tried & true recipes. She has been gone for many years, but my family still loves this tasty meal...and I love how simple it is to make.

Serves 4

2 T. oil
4 boneless, skinless chicken breasts, cut into bite-size
   pieces
1/2 t. salt
1 t. pepper
1 onion, diced

2 cubes chicken bouillon
2 c. boiling water
1 c. long-cooking rice, uncooked
1 t. lemon zest
1/2 t. dried marjoram
10-oz. pkg. frozen peas

Heat oil in a large skillet over medium heat. Season chicken with salt and pepper. Cook chicken in oil until golden on all sides. Add onion and sauté for 5 minutes, or until golden. Add bouillon, water and rice. Reduce heat to low. Cover and cook, stirring occasionally, for 25 minutes, or until rice is tender. Sprinkle lemon zest and marjoram over chicken mixture. Add peas; cover and cook over low heat for 10 minutes, or until peas are tender.

Chicken-Rice Skillet

Julie De Fusco, Las Vegas, NV

Pork Chops Olé

This was one of my favorite dishes to make when I was just learning to cook...it's so easy and so tasty. Make it spicier by adding a little chopped jalapeño.

Serves 4

2 T. oil
4 pork chops
2 T. butter
6.8-oz. pkg. Spanish-flavored rice vermicelli mix
14-1/2 oz. can Mexican-style stewed tomatoes
1-1/2 c. water
Garnish: sour cream, chopped fresh cilantro

Heat oil in a large skillet over medium heat. Cook pork chops in oil until browned on both sides, about 6 minutes; remove from skillet and keep warm. Melt butter in same skillet; add rice mix to butter. Cook and stir until rice mix is lightly golden. Stir in tomatoes with juice and water. Add pork chops to skillet and bring to a boil. Reduce heat to low; cover and cook for 20 to 30 minutes, until liquid is absorbed and pork chops are no longer pink in the center. Garnish with sour cream and cilantro.

Carrie Porder, Woonsocket, RI

Creamed Chicken on Toast

This recipe dates from many years ago, when my mother-in-law was a young girl and her mother needed an easy dinner to serve. My grandmother-in-law never really liked to cook much, so what she served was plain & simple. She lived to be well over 100, so her cooking could not have been too bad! My mother-in-law and I have both adapted it for our own families. Serve it over rice or noodles, if you like.

Serves 6 to 8

4 to 6 boneless, skinless chicken breasts, cut into
   bite-size pieces
1 onion, chopped
pepper and dried sage to taste
2 10-3/4 oz. cans cream of chicken soup
2 10-3/4 oz. cans cream of mushroom soup
2 10-3/4 oz. cans cream of celery soup
2 4-oz. cans mushroom stems and pieces, drained
2 4-oz. cans young peas, drained
Optional: salt to taste
4 to 8 slices bread, toasted

Place chicken in a lightly greased large stockpot; add onion, pepper and sage. Cover and cook over medium-high heat, stirring often, until chicken is no longer pink and juices run clear. If a thicker consistency is desired, drain juices from stockpot. Add soups, mushrooms and peas; stir well. Reduce heat to medium. Cook, stirring often, until heated through and flavors have blended, about 15 minutes. If desired, add salt to taste. Serve spooned over warm toast.

Vickie, Gooseberry Patch

Rosemary Chicken & Tomatoes

Tender, slow-simmered chicken at its best...I like to use the plum tomatoes and rosemary from my garden. It doesn't get any fresher than that!

Serves 5

1 T. oil
2 lbs. skinless chicken thighs
2/3 c. chicken broth
1/4 c. white wine or chicken broth
2 cloves garlic, minced
salt and pepper to taste
6 plum tomatoes, chopped
2 green peppers, cut into strips
1-1/2 c. sliced mushrooms
2 T. cornstarch
2 T. cold water
2 t. fresh rosemary, snipped
cooked egg noodles or rice

Heat oil in a skillet over medium heat. Sauté chicken in oil until golden, about 5 minutes; drain. Add broth, wine or broth, garlic, salt and pepper; bring to a boil. Reduce heat; cover and simmer for 20 minutes. Add tomatoes, peppers and mushrooms. Simmer, covered, for 15 minutes, or until chicken is cooked through. Transfer chicken to a serving dish and keep warm. In a small bowl, combine cornstarch, water and rosemary; stir into vegetable mixture. Cook and stir until thickened and bubbly. Serve chicken over noodles or rice; spoon sauce over chicken.

Peggy Donnally, Toledo, OH

Hamburger Gravy & Potatoes

My brother, Michael, has a big heart, an infectious laugh and the uncanny ability to turn childhood food memories into modern-day meals for his own family. This is his own tasty version of a quick dinner our mother used to make for us when we were young.

Serves 6

1-1/2 lbs. ground beef round
1 onion, finely chopped
1 t. onion powder
1/2 t. garlic powder
salt and pepper to taste
1/2 lb. sliced mushrooms
2 12-oz. jars beef gravy
mashed potatoes

Brown beef in a large skillet over medium heat; drain. Add onion and seasonings to skillet. Cook over medium-low heat until onion is translucent. Stir in mushrooms and gravy; cover and simmer for 10 minutes. Ladle over mashed potatoes.

Anita Mullins, *Eldridge, MO*

Anita's Onion Steaks

A simply delicious way to fix cube steaks! Serve them with mashed potatoes, cooked egg noodles or rice, with the gravy from the skillet ladled over all.

Serves 4

15-oz. can beef broth
Optional: 1/2 c. red wine
1.35-oz. pkg. onion soup mix
1 onion, thinly sliced
4 beef cube steaks
pepper to taste
10-3/4 oz. can cream of onion soup

In a skillet over medium heat, combine broth, wine, if using, and soup mix; mix well. Add onion and steaks; sprinkle with pepper to taste. Reduce heat to low; cover and simmer for 30 minutes. Turn steaks over; cover and simmer for an additional 30 minutes. Remove steaks to a plate; stir soup into mixture in skillet. Return steaks to skillet, being sure to coat each steak with gravy. Cover and simmer over low heat for 15 minutes.

Sandra Lee Smith, *Quartz Hill, CA*

Aunt Annie's Chicken Paprika

My Aunt Annie used to cook for several restaurants and cafes...this was one of her best dishes. We made sure to include it in the family cookbook we put together!

Serves 8

2 to 3 c. all-purpose flour
1 t. salt
1/4 t. pepper
4 lbs. chicken
oil for frying
3 onions, sliced
1 clove garlic, chopped
6 carrots, peeled and sliced
2 T. Hungarian paprika
2 c. water
3 cubes chicken bouillon
cooked spaetzle or egg noodles

Mix flour, salt and pepper in a plastic zipping bag. Add chicken pieces, 2 at a time, and toss to coat. Heat 2 tablespoons oil in a Dutch oven over medium-high heat. Sauté onions and garlic until tender; remove from pan and set aside. Add additional oil to about 1/2-inch deep. Add chicken to oil and cook, turning once, until golden on both sides; drain. Remove chicken to a plate and keep warm. Stir in remaining ingredients except spaetzle or noodles. Bring to a boil; return chicken to Dutch oven. Simmer, covered, for one hour over low heat, or until chicken juices run clear. Serve with spaetzle or noodles.

Flavor Booster

······· ✳ ·······

Chicken thighs may be used
in most recipes calling for
chicken breasts. They're
juicier, more flavorful and
budget-friendly too.

Aunt Annie's Chicken Paprika

Carol Lytle, *Columbus, OH*

Family-Favorite Pork Tacos

My kids liked to order tacos just like these at our neighborhood Mexican restaurant, so I recreated the recipe to make at home.

Serves 4

2 t. oil
1-lb. pork tenderloin, cubed
1 t. ground cumin
2 cloves garlic, minced
1 c. green or red salsa
Optional: 1/2 c. fresh cilantro, chopped
8 10-inch corn tortillas, warmed
Garnish: shredded lettuce, diced tomatoes, sliced
   avocado, sliced black olives, sour cream,
   shredded Cheddar cheese

Heat oil in a skillet over medium-high heat. Add pork and cumin; cook until golden on all sides and pork is no longer pink in the center, about 8 to 10 minutes. Add garlic and cook for one minute; drain. Stir in salsa and heat through; stir in cilantro, if using. Using 2 forks, shred pork. Fill warmed tortillas with pork mixture; garnish as desired.

Family-Favorite Pork Tacos

Wendy Jacobs, *Idaho Falls, ID*

Chicken Viennese

Serves 4 to 6

2 T. butter
3 lbs. chicken
2 carrots, peeled and sliced
2 tomatoes, chopped
1 onion, chopped
1 green pepper, chopped
4-oz. can sliced mushrooms, drained
1/2 c. chicken broth
salt and pepper to taste
1 T. all-purpose flour
3/4 c. sour cream
2 to 3 c. cooked rice or noodles

Melt butter in a large skillet over medium-high heat. Add chicken pieces; cook until golden on both sides, about 10 minutes. Add vegetables, broth, salt and pepper to skillet. Reduce heat to medium-low. Simmer for 30 to 35 minutes, until chicken juices run clear when pierced. Remove chicken and vegetables to a serving platter; set aside. Stir flour and sour cream into drippings in skillet. Cook and stir until mixture thickens; spoon over chicken. Serve with cooked rice or noodles.

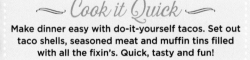

～ Cook it Quick ～

Make dinner easy with do-it-yourself tacos. Set out taco shells, seasoned meat and muffin tins filled with all the fixin's. Quick, tasty and fun!

Nicole Sampson, *Tiskilwa, IL*

Skillet Chicken-Fried Rice

This is a very easy one-skillet supper and it's oh-so delicious. Why order takeout when you can whip this up in no time flat?

Makes 4 servings

1 T. oil
2 eggs, beaten
1/2 c. frozen peas
1/2 c. carrot, peeled and sliced
1/4 c. onion, diced
2 c. cooked rice
1 c. cooked chicken, cubed
2 T. soy sauce
1 T. stir-fry sauce
1/4 t. garlic, minced

Heat oil in a large skillet over medium heat. Scramble eggs in oil. When eggs are set, remove from pan and chop. Lightly spray the same skillet with non-stick cooking spray and place over medium heat. Add peas, carrot and onion to skillet. Cook for 2 to 3 minutes, until vegetables are crisp-tender. Add chopped scrambled eggs and remaining ingredients to vegetable mixture. Cook, stirring occasionally, until mixture is heated through.

Angela Lengacher, *Montgomery, IN*

Fluffy Chicken & Dumplings

This is a wonderful way to warm up on a chilly night! Soft, fluffy dumplings in a warm & hearty mixture of chicken and vegetables...pure comfort food.

Serves 6

1 to 2 T. oil
1 c. celery, chopped
1 c. carrots, peeled and sliced
1 T. onion, chopped
49-oz. can chicken broth
10-3/4 oz. can cream of chicken soup
1/8 t. pepper
2 c. cooked chicken, cubed
1-2/3 c. biscuit baking mix
2/3 c. milk

Heat oil in a Dutch oven over medium-high heat. Sauté celery, carrots and onion in oil for about 7 minutes, until crisp-tender. Add broth, soup and pepper; bring to a boil. Reduce heat to low; stir in chicken and bring to a simmer. In a separate bowl, stir together baking mix and milk. Drop batter by tablespoonfuls into simmering broth. Cover and cook over low heat for 15 minutes without lifting lid.

Jo Ann, *Gooseberry Patch*

Picture-Perfect Paella

This classic Spanish dish is not only beautiful to look at, it's also amazingly delicious. It takes a little time to prepare, but it's so worth it.

Serves 8

3 lbs. chicken
2 onions, quartered
1 stalk celery, sliced
2 carrots, peeled and sliced
salt and pepper to taste
6 c. water
2 c. long-cooking rice, uncooked
2 cloves garlic, crushed
1/4 c. oil
1 c. peas
1/4 c. diced pimentos, drained
1/2 t. dried oregano
1/8 t. saffron or turmeric
1 lb. uncooked large shrimp, peeled and cleaned
12 uncooked clams in shells

In a large skillet over medium heat, combine chicken pieces, onions, celery, carrots, salt, pepper and water. Bring to a boil; reduce heat, cover and simmer for one hour. Remove vegetables and chicken, reserving 6 cups broth. Dice chicken and set meat aside, discarding bones. In the same skillet over medium heat, cook and stir rice and garlic in oil until golden. Add reserved chicken, reserved broth, peas, pimentos, oregano and saffron or turmeric. Cover and cook over low heat for 15 minutes. Add shrimp and clams; cover and cook for another 10 minutes, or until shrimp are pink and clams have opened.

Picture-Perfect Paella

Chapter Five

Easy Slow-Cooker Meals

Toss it in, turn it on...dinner is served! Why not let your slow cooker do the work for dinner tonight? Whether you're in the mood for a hearty bowl of Creamy Beef Stroganoff, or a couple of spicy BBQ Pulled-Pork Fajitas, your slow cooker is your best kitchen helper. From Magic Meatloaf to Best-Ever Lasagna, we bet you'll find lots of new family favorites!

Kelly Alderson, *Erie, PA*

Slow-Cooker Pepperoni Pizza

My kids can't get enough of this yummy pasta dish! Add sliced mushrooms, black olives and any other ingredients to make it just the way you like your pizza.

Serves 6

2 14-oz. jars pizza sauce
10-3/4 oz. can tomato soup
1-1/2 lbs. ground beef, browned and drained
8-oz. pkg. rigatoni pasta, cooked
16-oz. pkg. shredded mozzarella cheese
8-oz. pkg. sliced pepperoni

Mix together sauce and soup; set aside. Alternate layers in a slow cooker, using half each of beef, pasta, cheese, sauce mixture and pepperoni. Repeat layers. Cover and cook on low setting for 4 hours.

Janice Dorsey, *San Antonio, TX*

Sweet-and-Sour Pork

We really like this toss & go recipe...it's equally good with cubes of boneless chicken breast.

Makes 6 servings

1-1/2 lbs. boneless pork loin, cubed
1 green pepper, chopped
1 onion, chopped
14-oz. can pineapple chunks, drained
14-1/2 oz. can chicken broth
10-oz. bottle sweet-and-sour sauce
cooked rice

Place pork cubes in a slow cooker; top with remaining ingredients except rice. Cover and cook on low setting for 6 to 7 hours, or on high setting for 4 hours. Serve over cooked rice.

Lisanne Miller, *Canton, MS*

Italian Chicken Stew

This version is quicker than Grandma Oli's recipe, but it sure has the same great taste!

Makes 4 to 5 servings

3 to 4 boneless, skinless chicken breasts
2 28-oz. cans stewed tomatoes
20-oz. pkg. frozen Italian vegetables
1 clove garlic, minced
16-oz. pkg. rigatoni pasta, uncooked
Garnish: shredded mozzarella cheese, grated
   Parmesan cheese

Place chicken, tomatoes with juice, vegetables and garlic in a slow cooker. Cover and cook on low setting for 4 to 5 hours. About 35 minutes before cooking is complete, top stew with uncooked pasta; do not stir. Cover and finish cooking. Pasta will thicken the stew as it cooks. Garnish portions with cheeses.

~ *Handy Tip* ~
Keep a container in your freezer for leftover vegetables. When you are ready to make soup or stew, just add them...so handy!

Italian Chicken Stew

White Bean & Sausage Stew

Diane Cohen, *The Woodlands, TX*

White Bean & Sausage Stew

Add a basket of warm, buttered biscuits for a satisfying soup supper.

Serves 4

6 Italian pork sausage links
1/4 c. water
1 T. olive oil
1 onion, chopped
1 clove garlic, chopped
2 15-oz. cans Great Northern beans, drained
 and rinsed
28-oz. can chopped tomatoes, drained
1 t. dried thyme
salt and pepper to taste

Pierce sausages and place in a large skillet. Add water; bring to a boil over medium heat. Reduce heat and simmer for 10 minutes, turning occasionally. Transfer sausages to a plate. Heat oil in skillet over medium-high heat; sauté onion and garlic. Stir in beans, tomatoes and thyme. Add half of bean mixture to a slow cooker; arrange sausages on top. Spread remaining bean mixture over sausages. Cover and cook on high setting. Check after 2 hours; stir in additional water, if needed. Remove sausages; slice into thick chunks and return to slow cooker. Sprinkle with salt and pepper.

Angela Cradic, *Kingsport, TN*

Angela's Tortilla Stack

We like to think of this yummy dish as Mexican lasagna.

Makes 4 servings

1 lb. ground beef, browned and drained
5 to 6 6-inch corn tortillas, each cut into 6 wedges
10-3/4 oz. can Cheddar cheese soup
1-1/4 oz. pkg. taco seasoning mix
2 tomatoes, chopped
Garnish: sour cream, shredded lettuce

Crumble 1/4 of browned beef into the bottom of a slow cooker. Top with 1/4 of tortilla wedges. In a small bowl, blend soup and seasoning mix, using 2/3 to all of seasoning mix as desired. Spread 1/4 of soup mixture over tortillas. Sprinkle with 1/4 of tomatoes. Repeat layering until all ingredients are used. Cover and cook on low setting for 4 to 5 hours. Spoon onto individual plates. Top each serving with sour cream and lettuce as desired.

Jennifer Vallimont, *Kersey, PA*

Spicy Tortellini & Meatballs

This has to be one of my favorites for the slow cooker because it cooks for such a short time. When I don't have meatballs in the freezer, I have substituted browned and drained ground beef for the meatballs and it's just as tasty.

Makes 6 to 8 servings

14-oz. pkg. frozen cooked Italian meatballs, thawed
16-oz. pkg. frozen broccoli, cauliflower and carrot blend, thawed
2 c. cheese tortellini, uncooked
2 10-3/4 oz. cans cream of mushroom soup
2-1/4 c. water
1/2 to 1 t. ground cumin
salt and pepper to taste

Combine meatballs, vegetables and tortellini in a slow cooker. In a large bowl, whisk together soup, water and seasonings. Pour over meatball mixture; stir to combine well. Cover and cook on low setting for 3 to 4 hours.

Kathleen Poritz, *Burlington, WI*

Old-Fashioned Bean Soup

I'm a teacher's aide with winter recess duty...a cup of bean soup warms the body & soul!

Makes 8 to 10 servings

16-oz. pkg. dried navy beans
2 qts. water
1 meaty ham bone
1 onion, chopped
1/2 c. celery leaves, chopped
5 whole peppercorns
salt to taste
Optional: bay leaf

Cover beans with water in a large soup pot; soak overnight. Drain. Combine beans, 2 quarts water and remaining ingredients in a slow cooker. Cover and cook on low setting for 10 to 12 hours, or on high setting for 5 to 6 hours. Remove ham bone; dice meat and return to slow cooker. Discard bay leaf, if using. Serve with Easy Cornbread.

Easy Cornbread:

Makes 10 to 12 servings

8-1/2 oz. pkg. corn muffin mix
8-1/2 oz. pkg. yellow cake mix
2 eggs, beaten
1/3 c. milk
1/2 c. water

Combine all ingredients; mix well. Spread batter in a greased 13"x9" baking pan. Bake at 350 degrees for 15 to 20 minutes.

Old-Fashioned Bean Soup

Game-Day Corn Chowder

Jo Ann, *Gooseberry Patch*

Game-Day Corn Chowder

This savory chowder is always simmering away in my slow cooker on football Saturday mornings so it's ready to enjoy by kick-off.

Serves 6

1 lb. smoked pork sausage
3 c. frozen hashbrowns with onions and peppers
2 carrots, peeled and chopped
15-oz. can creamed corn
10-3/4 oz. can cream of mushroom soup with roasted garlic
2 c. water

Brown sausage in a skillet over medium heat; drain and cut into bite-size pieces. Place sausage in a slow cooker; top with hashbrowns and carrots. Combine corn, soup and water; stir until blended and pour over sausage mixture. Cover and cook on low setting for 8 to 10 hours.

Stephanie Westfall, *Dallas, GA*

Stephanie's Pepper Steak

A family favorite! Sprinkle with chow mein noodles if you like a crunchy topping.

Makes 4 to 6 servings

1-1/2 to 2 lbs. beef round steak, sliced into strips
15-oz. can diced tomatoes

1 to 2 red peppers, sliced
1 onion, chopped
4-oz. can sliced mushrooms, drained
1/4 c. salsa
cooked rice

Mix all ingredients except rice in a slow cooker. Cover and cook on low setting for 6 to 8 hours. To serve, spoon over cooked rice.

Evelyn Webb, *Chicago Heights, IL*

Italian Beef & Pasta

Two meals in one, because any leftover beef makes make great sandwiches the next day!

Serves 8 to 10

3 to 4-lb. beef chuck roast
2 onions, sliced
13-1/4 oz. can sliced mushrooms
2 26-oz. jars marinara pasta sauce
2 T. zesty Italian salad dressing mix
16-oz. pkg. spaghetti, cooked

Combine all ingredients except spaghetti in a slow cooker. Cover and cook on low setting for 8 hours. Slice beef; spoon sauce over cooked pasta and serve beef on the side.

~ Handy Tip ~

Always turn your slow cooker off, unplug it from the electrical outlet and allow it to cool before cleaning. The outside of the heating base may be cleaned with a soft cloth and warm soapy water.

Rita Morgan, *Pueblo, CO*

Smoky Beef Brisket

Tender slices of brisket with an amazing flavor.

Serves 4 to 6

2-1/2 lb. beef brisket, halved
1 T. smoke-flavored cooking sauce
1 t. salt
1/2 t. pepper
1/2 c. onion, chopped
1/2 c. catsup
2 t. Dijon mustard
1/2 t. celery seed

Rub brisket with smoke-flavored cooking sauce, salt and pepper; place in a slow cooker. Top with onion. Combine remaining ingredients; spread over brisket. Cover and cook on low setting for 8 to 9 hours. Remove brisket and keep warm. Transfer cooking juices to a blender; process until smooth. Serve with brisket.

Wendy West Hickey, *Pittsburgh, PA*

White Chili

Speed up this recipe by substituting canned beans... you'll need about three, 15-ounce cans. No soaking required!

Serves 6 to 8

16-oz. pkg. dried Great Northern beans
2 lbs. boneless, skinless chicken breasts, cubed
14-1/2 oz. can chicken broth
1 c. water
1 onion, chopped
3 cloves garlic, minced
2 4-oz. cans chopped green chiles
2 t. ground cumin

1-1/2 t. cayenne pepper
1 t. dried oregano
1/2 t. salt
Garnish: shredded Monterey Jack cheese, chopped
  green onions

Cover beans with water in a large soup pot and soak overnight; drain. In a slow cooker, combine beans with remaining ingredients except garnish and stir. Cover and cook on low setting for 10 to 12 hours, or on high setting for 5 to 6 hours, stirring occasionally. Garnish individual portions as desired.

Linda Neel, *Lovington, NM*

Green Chile Stew

Perfect for a cold evening! Use hot, medium or mild green chiles according to your own taste.

Serves 4

1 to 1-1/2 lbs. boneless pork, cubed
2 16-oz. cans pinto beans
2 14-1/2 oz. cans Mexican-style diced tomatoes
2 4-oz. cans diced green chiles
15-1/2 oz. can hominy, drained
1 t. ground cumin
salt and pepper to taste

Place pork in a slow cooker. Top with remaining ingredients; do not drain beans, tomatoes or chiles. Stir. Cover and cook on high setting for 4 to 5 hours.

Cook it Quick

Baked potatoes are yummy with any dish, and with a slow cooker, so easy to prepare. Simply use a fork to pierce 10 to 12 baking potatoes and wrap each in aluminum foil. Arrange them in a slow cooker, cover and cook on high setting for 2-1/2 to 4 hours, until tender.

Green Chile Stew

Southern BBQ Bean Soup

Tori Willis, *Champaign, IL*

Southern BBQ Bean Soup

When my daughter visited Alabama, this was one recipe she brought home...it's becoming a family favorite up north too!

Serves 6 to 8

16-oz. pkg. dried Great Northern beans
3/4 c. onion, chopped
1/8 t. pepper
2 lbs. beef short ribs, cut into serving-size pieces
6 c. water
1 c. barbecue sauce
1 to 2 t. salt

Cover beans with water in a large soup pot; soak overnight. Drain. Combine beans, onion, pepper and short ribs in a slow cooker; add enough water to cover. Cover and cook on low setting for 10 to 12 hours. Remove short ribs; cut meat from bones. Return meat to slow cooker; stir in sauce and salt to taste. Cover and cook on high setting for an additional 20 minutes, or until warmed through.

Rebecca Ruff, *Carthage, NY*

French Onion Pork Chops

Pork chops and apples pair up nicely...spoon some old-fashioned fried apples into bowls for an easy side dish.

Serves 4

4 pork chops
10-1/2 oz. can French onion soup
1/4 c. water
1 t. dried parsley
cooked egg noodles

Place pork chops in a slow cooker. Mix soup and water together; pour over pork. Sprinkle with parsley. Cover and cook on low setting for about 8 hours. Serve over hot cooked noodles.

Kathleen White, *Cato, NY*

Beef Tips & Gravy

All ten members of my family raved about this slow-cooker creation.

Serves 6 to 8

3 lbs. stew beef cubes
15-oz. can tomato sauce
2 c. water
1.35-oz. pkg. onion soup mix
1/3 c. instant tapioca, uncooked
1 to 2 t. beef bouillon granules
cooked egg noodles

Place beef in a slow cooker. Combine remaining ingredients except noodles; pour over beef. Cover and cook on low setting for 8 to 10 hours, or on high setting for 5 to 6 hours. Serve over cooked noodles.

⟨ *Handy Tip* ⟩

Do your favorite slow-cooker recipes finish cooking a few hours before you get home? If your slow cooker doesn't have a timer setting, then you may want to prepare the ingredients the night before. If you refrigerate the filled crock overnight, it will take 2 to 3 hours longer to cook, which is perfect when you will be out & about all day!

Lisa Ashton, *Aston, PA*

Tangy Beef & Noodles

There are so many flavors of barbecue sauce...from traditional tomato to fruit, mustard and vinegar. Try something new for a change each time you make this.

Serves 4 to 6

2 to 2-1/2 lbs. stew beef cubes
1 c. barbecue sauce
1 T. prepared horseradish
1 t. mustard
1/4 t. salt
1/8 t. pepper
cooked wide egg noodles

Place beef in a slow cooker. Combine barbecue sauce, horseradish, mustard, salt and pepper in a small bowl; pour over beef. Cover and cook on low setting for 7 to 8 hours. Arrange beef and sauce over cooked noodles.

Peggy Pelfrey, *Fort Riley, KS*

Chuck Wagon Stew

This hearty stew is ideal for a fall social or a weekend at the cabin.

Makes 6 servings

1-1/2 lbs. stew beef cubes
1/2 lb. smoked pork sausage, sliced
1 onion, chopped
3 potatoes, peeled and cubed
28-oz. can barbecue baked beans

Place beef, sausage, onion and potatoes into a slow cooker; mix well. Spoon beans over top. Cover and cook on low setting for 8 to 10 hours, or on high setting 4 to 5 hours. Stir again before serving.

Barb Sulser, *Delaware, OH*

Pork Chops & Scalloped Potatoes

Mom always made this, and it became a family favorite comfort food. You can flour and brown the pork chops before adding to the slow cooker, if you like.

Serves 6

1 onion, sliced, separated into rings and divided
8 potatoes, peeled, sliced and divided
16-oz. pkg. pasteurized process cheese spread, sliced and divided
6 boneless pork chops
salt and pepper to taste
10-3/4 oz. can cream of chicken soup

Spread a layer of onion rings in a slow cooker. Place a layer of potatoes over onion rings, then a layer of cheese. Continue to layer until slow cooker is 2/3 full. Sprinkle pork chops with salt and pepper; place on top. Spread soup over top. Cover and cook for 6 to 8 hours on low setting, or 3 to 4 hours on high setting.

> ～ *Handy Tip* ～
> Don't remove the slow-cooker lid unless you're checking for doneness or stirring. Every time the cover comes off, you lose heat that is equal to 30 minutes of cooking time, so trust the recipe!

Chuck Wagon Stew

Black Bean Chili

Darrell Lawry, *Kissimmee, FL*

Black Bean Chili

A different kind of chili! I like to top the bowl with a handful of crushed tortilla chips.

Serves 4 to 6

1-lb. pork tenderloin
3 15-1/2 oz. cans black beans, drained and rinsed
16-oz. jar chunky salsa
1/2 c. chicken broth
1 green pepper, chopped
1 onion, chopped
2 t. chili powder
1 t. ground cumin
1 t. dried oregano
Garnish: sour cream, diced tomatoes

Place pork in a lightly greased slow cooker; add remaining ingredients except garnish. Cover and cook on low setting for 8 hours, or on high setting for 4 hours. Shred pork; return to slow cooker. Garnish servings with dollops of sour cream and diced tomatoes.

Handy Tip

Here's a tip to determine if your vintage slow cooker still heats properly. Fill it 2/3 full of water, cover and cook on high setting for 4 hours. Then check the water's temperature with an instant-read thermometer...if it reads 180 degrees, the slow cooker is working properly.

Kerry Mayer, *Dunham Springs, LA*

Cajun Pot Roast

A flavorful roast that's savory and delicious.

Serves 6

2-lb. boneless beef chuck roast
1 T. Cajun seasoning
1 onion, chopped
14-1/2 oz. can diced tomatoes with garlic
1/2 t. hot pepper sauce
1/8 t. pepper

Sprinkle roast with Cajun seasoning; rub to coat. Place roast in a slow cooker; top with onion. Combine tomatoes with juice and remaining ingredients; pour over roast. Cover and cook on low setting for 8 to 10 hours.

Kim Workman, *Gastonia, NC*

Ham & Fixin's

A recipe passed along by a friend at work, this makes a great one-pot meal that's ready when you come home from work or to take to a friend. I love slow-cooker cooking!

Makes 6 to 8 servings

3 lbs. cooked ham, sliced
6 to 8 potatoes, peeled and diced
14-1/2 oz. can green beans
15-oz. can corn

Place ham in a slow cooker. Surround ham with cut potatoes; pour green beans with juices over top. Cover and cook on low setting for 8 hours. Pour corn with juices into slow cooker 2 hours before serving.

Sally Kohler, *Webster, NY*

Sally's Supreme Corned Beef

Use a little cornstarch to thicken the broth after removing the brisket...it makes really good gravy for the noodles.

Makes 4 to 6 servings

2 to 3-lb. corned beef brisket
12-oz. bottle chili sauce
1.35-oz. pkg. onion soup mix
12-oz. can cola
cooked egg noodles

Place brisket in slow cooker. Mix remaining ingredients except noodles; pour over brisket. Cover and cook on low setting for 6 to 8 hours. Slice beef and serve over noodles.

Brenda Smith, *Delaware, OH*

Mom's One-Pot Dinner

This has always been a warm-you-to-your-toes dinner our family enjoys after a chilly day outside.

Serves 6 to 8

1 head cabbage, shredded
3 potatoes, peeled and cubed
1 onion, chopped
1-3/4 t. salt
1/4 t. pepper
14-1/2 oz. can chicken broth
2 lbs. Kielbasa, cut into serving-size pieces

In a slow cooker, combine cabbage, potatoes, onion, salt and pepper; add broth. Place Kielbasa on top. Cover and cook on low setting for 8 to 9 hours.

Sue Neely, *Greenville, IL*

Down-on-the-Bayou Gumbo

You can't help but smile with a bowl of gumbo in front of you!

Serves 6

3 T. all-purpose flour
3 T. oil
3 c. chicken broth
1/2 lb. smoked pork sausage, sliced
2 c. frozen okra
14-1/2 oz. can diced tomatoes
1 onion, chopped
1 green pepper, chopped
3 cloves garlic, minced
1/4 t. cayenne pepper
3/4 lb. cooked medium shrimp, tails removed
cooked rice

Stir together flour and oil in a saucepan over medium heat. Cook, stirring constantly, for 5 minutes. Reduce heat; cook and stir for 10 minutes, or until mixture is reddish brown. Pour broth into a slow cooker; stir in flour mixture. Add remaining ingredients except shrimp and rice; do not drain tomatoes.. Cover and cook on low setting for 7 to 9 hours. Shortly before serving, add shrimp to slow cooker; mix well. Cover and cook on low setting for about 20 minutes. Ladle gumbo over cooked rice in soup bowls.

Down-on-the Bayou Gumbo

Grama's Minestrone Soup

Lori Czarnecki, *Milwaukee, WI*

Grama's Minestrone Soup

This is a recipe my grandmother used to make on the stovetop...I adapted it to the slow cooker.

Serves 6

14-1/2 oz. can diced tomatoes
15-1/2 oz. can kidney beans, drained and rinsed
2 14-oz. cans vegetable broth
3 c. water
1/4 c. zesty Italian salad dressing
1 c. onion, chopped
1/2 c. celery, chopped
1/2 c. carrot, peeled and chopped
1 t. Italian seasoning
1-1/2 c. small shell pasta, uncooked

Combine tomatoes with juice and remaining ingredients except pasta in a slow cooker; mix well. Cover and cook on low setting for 8 hours. Stir uncooked pasta into slow cooker. Cover and cook on high setting for an additional 30 minutes, or until pasta is tender.

Lisa Ashton, *Aston, PA*

Pine Cones in Tomato Sauce

No, they're not really pine cones, but tasty beef and rice balls!

Makes 4 servings

2 8-oz. cans tomato sauce
1/4 t. garlic powder
1/2 c. water
1-1/4 lbs. ground beef
1/2 c. long-cooking rice, uncooked
2 T. onion, chopped
1/2 t. salt
1/4 t. pepper

Mix together tomato sauce, garlic powder and water in a slow cooker. Combine remaining ingredients in a large bowl; mix well. Shape into 24 pine cone-shaped balls; arrange in slow cooker. Cover and cook on low setting for 7 to 8 hours.

~ *Handy Tip* ~

If you're buying ground beef or turkey in large quantities, why not use your slow cooker to brown it all at once? It will be ready for recipes whenever you need it! Just add up to 5 pounds of freshly ground meat to a large slow cooker; add some chopped onion if desired. Cover and cook on high setting for 2 to 2-1/2 hours, until brown, stirring every so often. Drain in a colander; cool and divide into freezer-ready portions.

Angela Couillard, *Lakeville, MN*

Sausage-Stuffed Squash

Sweet, savory and oh-so tender! This tasty squash is a welcome addition to a holiday supper, or serve it as a simple weeknight meal.

Makes 4 servings

14-oz. pkg. smoked pork sausage, diced
1/3 c. dark brown sugar, packed
1 T. butter-flavored sprinkles
1/4 t. dried sage
2 acorn squash, halved and seeded
1 c. water

In a bowl, mix together sausage, brown sugar, sprinkles and sage; toss to mix well. Fill squash halves heaping full with sausage mixture; wrap each stuffed half with aluminum foil. Pour water into a large slow cooker; place wrapped squash halves in slow cooker, stacking if necessary. Cover and cook on low setting for 6 to 8 hours.

Geneva Rogers, *Gillette, WY*

Baja Steak

The steak is so tender...turn any leftovers into amazing beef burritos for a cook-once, eat-twice dinner.

Serves 6

1-1/2 lbs. boneless beef round steak, cut into
   serving-size pieces
2 c. frozen corn, thawed and drained
18-oz. jar chunky garden salsa
15-oz. can black beans, drained and rinsed
1 onion, chopped
1/2 c. water
1/2 t. salt
Optional: 1/8 t. red pepper flakes

Place beef in a slow cooker. Mix remaining ingredients together; pour over beef. Cover and cook on low setting for 8 to 9 hours.

Claire Bertram, *Lexington, KY*

Beefy Mushroom Bake

Quick-cooking barley is a terrific pantry staple, and is so tasty in this slow-cooked dinner.

Serves 4 to 6

1 to 1-1/2 lbs. beef round steak, cubed
3/4 c. quick-cooking barley, uncooked
10-3/4 oz. can golden mushroom soup
2/3 c. water
3/4 lb. sliced mushrooms

Combine all ingredients in a slow cooker; mix well. Cover and cook on low setting for 7 to 8 hours.

Dale-Harriet Rogovich, *Madison, WI*

Chicken Noodle Soup

At the first sign of sniffles, I put this soup on to simmer. It makes me feel much better in no time!

Makes 8 servings

4 carrots, peeled and sliced
4 stalks celery, sliced
1 onion, chopped
2 bay leaves
1/2 t. dried thyme
4 t. salt
1/2 t. pepper
3-1/2 lb. chicken
7 to 8 c. chicken broth or water
3 c. medium egg noodles, uncooked

Place vegetables, seasonings and chicken in a slow cooker. Add enough broth or water to fill slow cooker 2/3 full. Cover and cook on low setting for 8 to 10 hours. Remove chicken and cool, reserving broth in slow cooker. Discard bones, skin and bay leaves. Stir uncooked noodles into slow cooker. Cover and cook on low setting for 10 to 20 minutes, until tender. Shred chicken and stir back into soup.

Jackie Valvardi, *Haddon Heights, NJ*

BBQ Pulled-Pork Fajitas

We like to spice these up with shredded Pepper Jack cheese, guacamole and sour cream.

Makes 18 servings

2-1/2 lb. boneless pork loin roast, trimmed
1 onion, thinly sliced

2 c. barbecue sauce
3/4 c. chunky salsa
1 T. chili powder
1 t. ground cumin
16-oz. pkg. frozen stir-fry peppers and onions
1/2 t. salt
18 8 to 10-inch flour tortillas, warmed

Place roast in a slow cooker; top with onion. Mix sauce, salsa and spices; pour over roast. Cover and cook on low setting for 8 to 10 hours. Remove roast and place on a cutting board; shred, using 2 forks. Return to slow cooker and mix well; add stir-fry vegetables and salt. Increase setting to high; cover and cook for an additional 30 minutes, or until hot and vegetables are tender. With a slotted spoon, fill each warmed tortilla with 1/2 cup pork mixture.

Marcel Beers, *Easton, PA*

Everyone's Favorite Vegetable Soup

Like a vegetable garden in a soup bowl...even my one-year-old likes it!

Makes 8 servings

1 lb. stew beef cubes
1 T. oil
4 potatoes, peeled and diced
16-oz. pkg. frozen peas
16-oz. pkg. frozen corn
16-oz. pkg. baby carrots
2 12-oz. jars beef gravy
2 15-oz. cans tomato sauce
salt and pepper to taste

In a skillet over medium heat, brown beef in oil; drain. Add potatoes to skillet; cook until softened. Combine beef mixture and remaining ingredients in a slow cooker. Cover and cook on low setting for 8 hours, or until tender, stirring occasionally.

Estella Hickman, *Galloway, OH*

Savory Chicken Soup

Oh, how the aroma of this simmering soup fills the kitchen!

Serves 4 to 6

2 carrots, peeled and sliced
2 stalks celery, chopped
2 to 3 potatoes, peeled and quartered
2 onions, sliced
3 boneless, skinless chicken breasts, cubed
14-1/2 oz. can chicken broth
2 c. water
1/4 t. salt
1/4 t. pepper
1/2 t. dried parsley
1/2 t. dried basil

Place vegetables in a slow cooker; add chicken. Pour in broth and water; sprinkle seasonings over top. Cover and cook on low setting for 8 hours, or on high setting for 4 hours.

Savory Chicken Soup

Anne's Chicken Burritos

Jennifer Sievers, Roselle, IL

Anne's Chicken Burritos

My friend, Anne, gave me this easy slow-cooker recipe...we love it more and more each time we make it!

Serves 6 to 8

6 boneless, skinless chicken breasts
15-1/4 oz. can corn, drained
16-oz. can black beans, drained and rinsed
16-oz. jar salsa
6 to 8 10-inch flour tortillas
Garnish: shredded Cheddar cheese, sour cream, salsa, guacamole

Place chicken in a slow cooker; top with corn, beans and salsa. Cover and cook on low setting for 8 to 10 hours, or on high setting for 4 to 6 hours. Shred chicken; stir back into slow cooker. To serve, spoon mixture onto tortillas. Add desired garnishes and roll up.

Simple Swap
.... * ....

Serve burritos in flavorful wraps for a tasty change. There are so many flavors...try Pepper-Jack cheese, spinach, tomato-basil and salsa.

Kathi Downey, Lompoc, CA

Sloppy Joe Chicken

Super for any game-day meal...it cooks up while you're waiting for the next touchdown!

Serves 4

6 skinless chicken thighs
8-oz. can tomato sauce
1-1/2 oz. pkg. Sloppy Joe mix
2 T. honey
cooked rice

Place chicken in a slow cooker. Combine remaining ingredients except rice; pour over chicken. Cover and cook on low setting for 6 hours. Discard bones. Serve chicken and sauce over cooked rice.

Erin Neuhaus, *Lincoln, NE*

Special Beef Fajitas

*These are always a favorite for casual dinner parties...
the slow cooker does all the work!*

Makes 8 to 10 servings

1-1/2 lbs. beef round steak
14-1/2 oz. can diced tomatoes, drained
1 onion, sliced
1 green pepper, sliced into strips
1 red pepper, sliced into strips
1 jalapeño, chopped
2 cloves garlic, minced
1 t. fresh cilantro, chopped
1 t. chili powder
1 t. ground cumin
1 t. ground coriander
1/4 t. salt
8 to 10 6-inch flour tortillas
Garnish: sour cream, guacamole, salsa, shredded
  Cheddar cheese, shredded lettuce

Place beef in a slow cooker. Combine vegetables and seasonings; spoon over beef. Cover and cook on low setting for 8 to 10 hours, or on high setting for 4 to 5 hours. Shred beef; serve with a slotted spoon on tortillas. Add favorite toppings; roll up tortillas.

Judy Schlosser, *Shubert, NE*

Calico Beans

*This is an old family favorite, requested at all
of our family reunions.*

Serves 20

2 lbs. ground beef, browned and drained
1/2 to 1 lb. bacon, crisply cooked and crumbled
1 onion, chopped
3 15-oz. cans pork & beans
2 16-oz. cans kidney beans
2 16-oz. cans baby butter beans
16-oz. can navy beans
1 c. catsup
1/2 c. brown sugar, packed
2 T. prepared horseradish
2 T. Worcestershire sauce
hot pepper sauce to taste

Add all ingredients to a slow cooker; do not drain beans. Mix well. Cover and cook on low setting for 6 hours. Stir again before serving.

Calico Beans

Joan's Chicken Stuffing Casserole

Beth Schlieper, *Lakewood, CO*

Kielbasa & Red Beans

Serve over bowls of rice for traditional red beans & rice.

Serves 6 to 8

1 lb. Kielbasa, cut into bite-size pieces
4 to 5 16-oz. cans red beans, drained and rinsed
2 14-1/2 oz. cans diced tomatoes
1 onion, chopped
hot pepper sauce to taste

Combine all ingredients in a slow cooker. Cover and cook on low setting for 8 hours, or on high setting for 4 to 5 hours.

Joan Brochu, *Harwich, MA*

Joan's Chicken Stuffing Casserole

Hearty and so filling, this chicken dish will be the first to disappear at any potluck.

Serves 6

12-oz. pkg. chicken stuffing mix
3 10-3/4 oz. cans cream of chicken soup, divided
1/2 c. milk
3 to 4 c. cooked chicken, cubed
12-oz. pkg. shredded Cheddar cheese

Prepare stuffing mix according to package directions; place in a slow cooker. Stir in 2 cans soup. In a separate bowl, stir together remaining soup, milk and chicken. Add to slow cooker. Spread cheese over top. Cover and cook on low setting for 4 to 6 hours, or on high setting for 2 to 3 hours.

Dana Cunningham, *Lafayette, LA*

Mom's Black-Eyed Pea Soup

This is one recipe sure to be found in every recipe box in our family.

Makes 6 servings

16-oz. pkg. dried black-eyed peas
10-3/4 oz. can bean with bacon soup
4 c. water
6 carrots, peeled and chopped
2-lb. beef chuck roast, cubed
1/4 t. pepper

Combine dried peas and remaining ingredients in a slow cooker; mix well. Cover and cook on low setting for 9 to 10 hours.

Betty Kozlowski, *Newnan, GA*

Easy Chili Rellenos

My husband fell in love with this the first time he tasted it! It's a potluck pleaser too.

Serves 6

2 t. butter
7-oz. can whole green chiles, drained and cut in strips
8-oz. pkg. shredded Cheddar cheese
8-oz. pkg. shredded Monterey Jack cheese
14-1/2 oz. can stewed tomatoes
4 eggs, beaten
2 T. all-purpose flour
3/4 c. evaporated milk

Spread butter in a slow cooker. Layer chiles and cheeses; add tomatoes with juice. Stir together eggs, flour and milk; pour into slow cooker. Cover and cook on high setting for 2 to 3 hours.

Peggy Donnally, *Toledo, OH*

Sunday Beef & Noodles

Noodles and potatoes with beef gravy...that's my idea of heaven on a plate!

Serves 6

2-lb. beef chuck roast
4 c. beef broth
1 c. onion, chopped
2 t. onion powder
1 t. garlic powder
1 T. dried parsley
salt and pepper to taste
16-oz. pkg. extra-wide egg noodles, cooked
mashed potatoes

Place roast in a slow cooker. Combine broth, onion and seasonings; pour over roast. Cover and cook on low setting for 6 to 8 hours. Remove roast; slice and return to slow cooker. Add noodles to slow cooker; heat through. Serve over mashed potatoes, with Glazed Carrots on the side.

Glazed Carrots:

Serves 6

16-oz. pkg. baby carrots
1/2 c. orange juice
5 T. brown sugar, packed
2 T. butter
1/8 t. salt

Cover carrots with water in a saucepan. Cook until tender; drain. Add juice to saucepan; simmer until almost evaporated. Stir in remaining ingredients; cook until well blended and glazed.

Sunday Beef & Noodles

Provincial Chicken

Shari Upchurch, *Dearing, GA*

Provincial Chicken

I've tweaked this recipe over the years...now it's just the way my family likes it!

Serves 6

4 boneless, skinless chicken breasts
2 15-oz. cans diced tomatoes
2 zucchini, diced
10-3/4 oz. can cream of chicken soup
2 T. balsamic vinegar
1 T. dried, minced onion
2 T. dried parsley
1 t. dried basil
1 c. shredded Cheddar cheese
1/2 c. sour cream
cooked bowtie pasta

In a slow cooker, combine chicken, tomatoes with juice, zucchini, soup, vinegar, onion and herbs. Cover and cook on low setting for 6 to 8 hours. Remove chicken; cut into bite-size pieces and return to slow cooker. Stir in cheese and sour cream; cover and cook for an additional 15 minutes. To serve, spoon over cooked pasta.

Linda Wolfe, *Westminster, CO*

Colorado Pork Chops

These tasty pork chops feature all the flavors of your favorite Mexican restaurant.

Serves 6

6 bone-in pork chops, 1-1/2 inches thick
15-oz. can chili beans with chili sauce
1-1/2 c. salsa
1 c. corn
Optional: green chiles to taste
cooked rice
Garnish: chopped fresh cilantro

In a slow cooker, layer pork chops, beans, salsa, corn and chiles, if using. Cover and cook on low setting for 5 hours, or on high setting for 2-1/2 hours. Serve over cooked rice; garnish with cilantro.

Stephanie Lucius, *Powder Springs, GA*

Southern Chicken & Dumplings

A scrumptious-tasting homemade dish...with almost no effort!

Serves 6 to 8

3 10-3/4 oz. cans cream of chicken soup
1/4 c. onion, diced
6 boneless, skinless chicken breasts
3-3/4 c. water
3 12-oz. tubes refrigerated biscuits, quartered

Pour soup into a slow cooker; add onion and chicken. Pour in enough water to cover chicken. Cover and cook on low setting for 6 to 8 hours, or on high setting for 4 to 6 hours. About 45 minutes before serving, turn slow cooker to high setting. Remove chicken with a slotted spoon; shred into bite-size pieces and return to slow cooker. Drop biscuit quarters into slow cooker; stir well. Replace lid and cook for 35 minutes more, or until dumplings are done. Stir and serve.

Wendy Sensing, *Brentwood, TN*

Pot Roast & Dumplings

This is one of our favorite meals on a chilly day...at the end of a busy day, dinner is practically ready!

Serves 8 to 10

2 c. baby carrots
5 potatoes, peeled and halved
4-lb. beef chuck roast
garlic salt and pepper to taste
2 c. water
1-oz. pkg. onion soup mix

Place carrots and potatoes in a slow cooker. Place roast on top; sprinkle with garlic salt and pepper. Stir together water and soup mix; pour over roast. Cover and cook on low setting for 6 to 8 hours. Drain most of broth from slow cooker into a large soup pot; bring to a boil over medium-high heat. Drop dumpling batter into boiling broth by teaspoonfuls. Cover and cook for 15 minutes. Serve roast with dumplings and vegetables.

Dumplings:

2 c. all-purpose flour
1/2 t. salt
3 T. baking powder
1 c. light cream

Sift together dry ingredients. Add cream and stir quickly to make a medium-soft batter.

Flavor Booster
························ ✳ ························
Good gravy...it's easy! Remove the cooked meat from the slow cooker, leaving juices inside. Make a smooth paste of 1/4 cup cold water and 1/4 cup cornstarch. Pour into the slow cooker, stir well and turn to high setting. Cook for 15 minutes once the mixture comes to a boil. Stir again before serving.

Pot Roast & Dumplings

Maxie Martin, *Granbury, TX*

Hearty Beef Stew

The night before, I do all the peeling and chopping, cover the potatoes with water and place in the fridge until morning.

Serves 8 to 10

6 potatoes, peeled and cubed
6 carrots, peeled and cut into 3-inch pieces
3 lbs. stew beef, cut into 1-1/2 inch cubes
1/3 c. soy sauce
1 t. paprika
1 t. salt
1/2 t. pepper
3 T. all-purpose flour
12-oz. pkg. frozen chopped onions
10-1/2 oz. can beef broth
8-oz. can tomato sauce

Arrange potatoes in a slow cooker; top with carrots. Add beef; sprinkle with soy sauce, seasonings, flour and onions. Combine broth and tomato sauce; pour over top. Cover and cook for 9 to 10 hours on low setting, or 4-1/2 to 5 hours on high setting.

Sharon Crider, *Junction City, KS*

Beans & Weenies

A year 'round favorite...a standby for summer picnics, yet hearty and satisfying during cold weather too!

Makes 6 to 8 servings

1 lb. hot dogs, sliced
3 16-oz. cans pork & beans
1/4 c. onion, chopped
1/2 c. catsup
1/4 c. molasses
2 t. mustard

Combine all ingredients in a slow cooker; stir well. Cover and cook on low setting for 3 to 4 hours.

Shelly Smith, *Dana, IN*

Creamy Beef Stroganoff

A midwestern favorite!

Serves 6 to 8

2 lbs. stew beef cubes
salt and pepper to taste
2 10-3/4 oz. cans cream of mushroom soup
3 T. Worcestershire sauce
3-oz. pkg. cream cheese, cubed
16-oz. container sour cream
cooked rice or noodles

Place beef in a slow cooker; sprinkle with salt and pepper. Pour soup over top; add Worcestershire sauce. Cover and cook on low setting for 8 to 10 hours. Stir in cream cheese and sour cream 30 minutes before serving. Serve over rice or noodles.

Rachel Boyd, *Defiance, OH*

Rachel's Turkey Stew

I combined 2 recipes to make this wonderful stew. Now it's a family favorite...even the kids love it!

Serves 6 to 8

28-oz. can turkey, drained and broth reserved
8-1/2 oz. can corn, drained and liquid reserved
1-1/2 c. frozen sliced carrots, thawed
14-1/2 oz. can chicken broth
1 c. buttermilk
1 T. dill weed
1/4 c. cornstarch

Mix together turkey, corn and carrots in a slow cooker; set aside. Whisk together reserved turkey broth, chicken broth, reserved corn liquid, buttermilk and dill weed; pour over turkey mixture. Cover and cook on low setting for 6 hours. Just before serving, stir in cornstarch and cook until thickened.

Jude Trimnal, *Brevard, NC*

Down-Home Pea Soup

Our parents made this soup often. It is delicious year 'round, but is especially warming on winter days.

Makes 8 to 10 servings

8 c. water
2 c. dried split peas
1-1/2 c. celery, sliced
1-1/2 c. carrots, peeled and sliced
1 onion, sliced
2 bay leaves
salt and pepper to taste
1 to 2 c. cooked ham, cubed

Combine all ingredients in a slow cooker. Cover and cook on low setting for 4 to 6 hours. Discard bay leaves before serving.

Lisa Sett, *Thousand Oaks, CA*

Chipotle Shredded Beef

My family asks for this often...it smells so good while it's cooking! Add a side of beans, and dinner is served.

Makes 6 to 8 servings

2-1/2 lb. beef chuck roast, trimmed
14-oz. can diced tomatoes
7-oz. can chipotle sauce
4-oz. can diced green chiles
1 onion, chopped
2 T. chili powder
1 t. ground cumin
2 c. beef broth
salt and pepper to taste
6 to 8 6-inch corn tortillas, warmed
Garnish: shredded Cheddar cheese, shredded lettuce,
    sliced black olives, chopped tomato

Place roast in a slow cooker. Top with undrained tomatoes and remaining ingredients except tortillas and garnish. Cover and cook on low setting for 8 to 10 hours. With 2 forks, shred roast in slow cooker; stir well. Spoon into warmed tortillas; add desired garnishes.

Sherry Doherty, *Medford, NJ*

German Roast Pork & Sauerkraut

A delicious one-pot dinner for New Year's Day or any time of year.

Serves 4 to 6

3 to 4-lb. boneless pork roast
salt and pepper to taste
1 T. shortening
32-oz. pkg. sauerkraut
2 apples, peeled, cored and quartered
1 c. apple juice or water
14-oz. pkg. frozen pierogies

Sprinkle roast with salt and pepper. Heat shortening in a skillet over medium-high heat. Brown roast on all sides; place in a slow cooker. Add undrained sauerkraut, apples and juice or water; blend. Gently add pierogies so they are partly submerged in the sauerkraut (as the roast cooks, more liquid will cover the pierogies). Cover and cook on low setting for 8 to 9 hours.

~ *Handy Tip* ~
Slow-cook an extra-large roast for 2 tasty meals in one...enjoy roast pork or beef the first night, then serve shredded meat with barbecue sauce on buns the next night!

Dawn Dhooghe, *Concord, NC*

Bayou Chicken

The slow cooker always seems to be going at our house. This is one of my husband's favorites...and it's so easy to put together!

Serves 6 to 8

3 boneless, skinless chicken breasts, cubed
14-1/2 oz. can chicken broth
14-1/2 oz. can diced tomatoes
10-3/4 oz. can tomato soup
1/2 lb. smoked pork sausage, sliced
1/2 c. cooked ham, diced
1 onion, chopped
2 t. Cajun seasoning
hot pepper sauce to taste
cooked rice

Combine all ingredients except rice in a slow cooker; stir. Cover and cook on low setting for 8 hours. Serve over cooked rice.

Beverly Tierney, Greenfield, IN

Magic Meatloaf

This is such a comforting dish and so nice to come home to. The meatloaf is so very flavorful and juicy... really wonderful!

Serves 4 to 6

2 lbs. ground beef
1 egg, beaten
1/2 c. green pepper, chopped
1/2 c. onion, chopped
1 c. milk
1 c. saltine cracker crumbs
.87-oz. pkg. brown gravy mix
1-1/2 t. salt
6 to 8 new redskin potatoes

Mix all ingredients except potatoes in a large bowl. Mix well and form into a loaf; place in a lightly greased slow cooker. Arrange potatoes around meatloaf. Cover and cook on low setting for 8 to 10 hours, or on high setting for 3 to 5 hours.

Cherylann Smith, Efland, NC

Best-Ever Lasagna

This is a quick, easy recipe for homestyle lasagna... just add garlic bread and a tossed salad.

Serves 6 to 8

1 lb. ground beef, browned and drained
1 t. Italian seasoning
8 lasagna noodles, uncooked and broken into thirds
28-oz. jar spaghetti sauce
1/3 c. water
4-oz. can sliced mushrooms, drained
15-oz. container ricotta cheese
8-oz. pkg. shredded mozzarella cheese
Garnish: shredded Parmesan cheese

Combine ground beef and Italian seasoning. Arrange half of the lasagna noodles in a greased slow cooker. Spread half of the ground beef mixture over noodles. Top with half each of remaining ingredients except Parmesan cheese. Repeat layering process. Cover and cook on low setting for 5 hours. Garnish with Parmesan cheese.

∽ Cook it Quick ∽

Stir cubes of leftover meatloaf into spaghetti sauce and serve over noodles...a tasty meal in minutes!

Best-Ever Lasagna

Corned Beef Dinner

Karen Alexander, *Navarre, OH*

Corned Beef Dinner

Delicious any time of the year...so easy to prepare in a slow cooker!

Serves 6 to 8

4 c. hot water
2 T. cider vinegar
1 c. carrots, peeled and sliced
1 onion, cut in wedges
1/2 t. pepper
3-lb. corned beef brisket with spice packet
8 redskin potatoes, quartered
1 head cabbage, cut into wedges

In a slow cooker, combine water, vinegar, carrots, onion and pepper. Top with brisket, contents of spice packet, potatoes and cabbage. Cover and cook on low setting for 8 to 10 hours.

Diana Chaney, *Olathe, KS*

Sunday Pork Roast Dinner

There's nothing like coming home from Sunday meetings to find a dinner that's ready to enjoy.

Serves 8

2 apples, peeled, cored and chopped
1 onion, chopped
3 T. honey mustard
2-lb. boneless pork roast
1/4 t. salt
1/4 t. pepper
2 T. cold water
1 T. cornstarch

Combine apples and onion in a slow cooker; set aside. Spread mustard over pork roast; sprinkle with salt and pepper. Place roast on top of apple mixture. Cover and cook on low setting for 7 to 8 hours. Remove roast to a platter, reserving mixture in slow cooker; cover with aluminum foil to keep warm. Whisk together water and cornstarch in a saucepan over medium heat. Add liquid, apples and onion from slow cooker. Cook until mixture boils and thickens, stirring frequently. Serve roast with sauce.

Jeanie Petersen, *Saint Charles, IL*

Cran-Orange Turkey Breast

My son requested a slow cooker primarily for this recipe! He has also shared the recipe as well as the meal with friends.

Serves 6

3 to 4-lb. boneless turkey breast
1/2 c. orange juice
1.35-oz. pkg. onion soup mix
15-oz. can whole-berry cranberry sauce

Place turkey breast in a slow cooker. Combine remaining ingredients; pour over turkey. Cover and cook on high setting for one hour; reduce to low setting and cook for an additional 5 to 6 hours.

Zoe Groff, *Saybrook, IL*

Pepper Steak

This hearty dish is sure to be a hit at any party...and they'll never know it only took you 10 minutes to put it together!

Makes 4 to 6 servings

1 to 1-1/2 lbs. beef round steak, cut into bite-size pieces
1/3 c. all-purpose flour
1/4 t. pepper
1 onion, sliced
1 green and/or red pepper, sliced
14-1/2 oz. can diced tomatoes
4-oz. can sliced mushrooms, drained
3 T. soy sauce
cooked rice

Place roast in a slow cooker. Sprinkle with flour and pepper; stir well to coat roast. Add remaining ingredients except rice. Cover and cook on high setting for one hour; reduce to low setting and cook for an additional 8 hours. Serve over cooked rice.

Marlene Darnell, *Newport Beach, CA*

Country Captain

We discovered this curry-flavored dish with the unusual name on a trip to southern Georgia.

Makes 4 servings

2 T. olive oil
3-lb. chicken, quartered and skin removed
2 cloves garlic, minced
1 onion, chopped
1 green pepper, chopped
1/2 c. celery, chopped
2 t. curry powder
1/3 c. currants or raisins
14-1/2 oz. can whole tomatoes, chopped
1 t. sugar
salt and pepper to taste
cooked rice
Garnish: 1/4 c. slivered almonds

Heat oil in a skillet over medium heat. Sauté chicken just until golden; place in a slow cooker and set aside. Add garlic, onion, green pepper, celery and curry powder to skillet; sauté briefly. Remove from heat; stir in remaining ingredients except rice and almonds. Pour over chicken. Cover and cook on low setting for 6 hours. Serve over cooked rice; sprinkle with almonds.

Country Captain

Pintos & Pork Over Corn Chips

Susan Butters, *Bountiful, UT*

Pintos & Pork Over Corn Chips

A hearty dish that feeds a crowd of hungry people... easily!

Makes 10 servings

16-oz. pkg. dried pinto beans
3-lb. pork loin roast, trimmed
7 c. water
4-oz. can chopped green chiles
1/2 c. onion, chopped
2 cloves garlic, minced
2 T. chili powder
1 T. ground cumin
1 T. salt
1 t. dried oregano
Garnish: corn chips, sour cream, shredded Cheddar
    cheese, chopped tomatoes, shredded lettuce

Cover beans with water in a large soup pot; soak overnight. Drain. Add beans and remaining ingredients except garnish to a slow cooker. Cover and cook on low setting for 9 hours. Remove roast, discarding bones; return to slow cooker. Cook, uncovered, for 30 minutes, until thickened. Serve over corn chips; garnish as desired.

Alicia Palmer, *Greenville, OH*

Down-Home Chicken & Noodles

My family just loves this dish...it tastes like you've been cooking all day!

Serves 6

1 lb. boneless, skinless chicken breasts
salt and pepper to taste
2 10-3/4 oz. cans cream of chicken soup
14-1/2 oz. can chicken broth
16-oz. pkg. wide egg noodles, cooked

Place chicken in a slow cooker; sprinkle with salt and pepper. Top with soup. Cover and cook on low setting for 6 hours, or until chicken is very tender. Remove chicken from slow cooker and shred; return to slow cooker. Add broth and cooked noodles; mix well. Cover and cook on low setting for an additional 30 minutes, or until heated through.

Chapter Six

Delightful Desserts

Cobblers, crisps, cakes...and more! Dinner just isn't complete without a sweet treat, and Grandma's Peach Cobbler is comfort food at its finest. Chocolate lovers will swoon over Triple Chocolate Cake and Double Chocolate Brownies. Don't forget to try the Spicy Pumpkin Raisin Cake...it's out of this world!

Phyllis Peters, *Three Rivers, MI*

Mix-in-a-Pan Nut Cake

So simple to stir up...just right with a pot of coffee and a good friend.

Serves 8 to 10

1/2 c. margarine
6-oz. jar strained carrot baby food
1 c. crushed pineapple with juice
1 egg, beaten
1 c. sugar
1-1/4 c. all-purpose flour
1 t. baking soda
2 t. cinnamon
1 t. vanilla extract
1 c. chopped English walnuts

Melt margarine in a 9"x9" baking pan. Gradually add remaining ingredients to pan; blend well. Bake at 325 degrees for 35 to 40 minutes.

Katie Majeske, *Denver, PA*

Praline Apple Crisp

What's more comforting than warm apple crisp? I often make this for work, church, potlucks or family.

Makes 10 servings

6 Granny Smith or Braeburn apples, peeled, cored
  and sliced
1 t. cinnamon
1/2 c. quick-cooking oats, uncooked
1/3 c. brown sugar, packed
1/4 c. all-purpose flour
1/2 c. chilled butter, diced
1/2 c. chopped pecans
1/2 c. toffee baking bits
Optional: whipped topping

Toss together apples and cinnamon. Place in a slow cooker that has been sprayed with non-stick vegetable spray; set aside. Combine oats, brown sugar, flour and butter; mix with a pastry cutter or fork until crumbly. Stir in pecans and toffee bits; sprinkle over apples. Cover and cook on low setting for 4 to 6 hours. Top with whipped topping, if desired.

Flavor Booster

.... ✳ ....

Butter-flavored non-stick
vegetable spray is handy at
dessert time. Spritz it on a
baking pan in a jiffy, adding
more flavor without
extra calories.

Praline Apple Crisp

Grandma's Peach Cobbler

Wendell Mays, *Barboursville, WV*

Grandma's Peach Cobbler

This is an awesome recipe, one my grandmother made very often. We could eat it daily! The almond extract and sprinkle of cinnamon were Grandma's special touches. A great comfort food that's so simple, any honeymooner could make it.

Serves 6 to 8

1/2 c. butter, sliced
15-1/4 oz. can sliced peaches in syrup
1 c. self-rising flour
1 c. sugar
1 c. milk
1 t. almond extract
cinnamon to taste
Optional: whipping cream or vanilla ice cream

Add butter to an 11"x7" baking pan; melt in a 350-degree oven. Pour peaches with syrup into pan; set aside. In a bowl, combine flour, sugar, milk and extract; stir until smooth. Pour batter over peaches. Bake at 350 degrees until bubbly and golden, about 35 to 45 minutes. Remove from oven; immediately sprinkle with cinnamon. Serve warm, topped with cream or ice cream, if desired.

Joan Brochu, *Harwich, MA*

Triple Chocolate Cake

This ooey-gooey dessert is a chocolate lover's delight!

Makes 8 to 10 servings

18-1/2 oz. pkg. chocolate cake mix
8-oz. container sour cream
3.9-oz. pkg. instant chocolate pudding mix
12-oz. pkg. semi-sweet chocolate chips
4 eggs, beaten
3/4 c. oil
1 c. water
Garnish: vanilla ice cream

Place all ingredients except ice cream in a slow cooker; mix well. Cover and cook on high setting for 3 to 4 hours. Serve warm, garnished with scoops of ice cream.

Kelly Rincan, *Manchester, NH*

Mom's Apple Pie

Mom used to make this pie for my family ever since I was a little girl. It reminds me of my family being together, all seven of us. I have now started the tradition with my own family...they love it! With a batter topping and no bottom crust, it's a snap to make.

Makes 6 to 8 servings

5 to 6 Cortland or Granny Smith apples, peeled, cored
   and sliced
1 t. cinnamon
1 c. plus 1 T. sugar, divided
1 c. all-purpose flour
3/4 c. butter, melted and slightly cooled
1 egg, beaten
1/8 t. salt
Optional: 1/2 c. chopped walnuts

Arrange apple slices in a greased 9" or 10" pie plate, filling 3/4 full. Sprinkle with cinnamon and one tablespoon sugar; set aside. In a bowl, mix together remaining sugar and other ingredients; pour over apples. Bake at 350 degrees for 50 minutes, or until golden and apples are tender.

Beth Kramer, *Port Saint Lucie, FL*

Tahitian Rice Pudding

Scrumptious served warm or cold.

Makes 6 to 8 servings

3/4 c. long-cooking rice, uncooked
15-oz. can cream of coconut
12-oz. can evaporated milk
2-3/4 c. water
Optional: 1 T. dark rum
2/3 c. sweetened flaked coconut

In a slow cooker, stir rice, cream of coconut, evaporated milk and water until combined. Cover and cook on low setting for 4 to 5 hours. Remove crock from slow cooker. Stir in rum, if using. Let pudding cool for 10 minutes. Heat a small non-stick skillet over medium heat. Add coconut; cook and stir for 4 to 5 minutes, until toasted. Transfer coconut to a plate. Spoon pudding into dessert bowls; sprinkle with coconut.

~ *Handy Tip* ~
If you've made too much rice, it's no problem.
Keep it on hand for yummy rice puddings, savory
casseroles, soups or stuffings.

Tahitian Rice Pudding

Microwave Cherry Crisp Cobbler

Jean Tillotson, *Sanford, NC*

Microwave Cherry Crisp Cobbler

Serve warm, topped with vanilla ice cream...out of this world!

Makes 8 servings

14-1/2 oz. can cherry pie filling
18-1/2 oz. pkg. white cake mix
2 T. brown sugar, packed
1 t. cinnamon
1/2 c. chopped pecans
1/2 c. margarine, melted

Spread cherry pie filling in an 8"x8" glass baking pan; set aside. Combine dry cake mix, brown sugar, cinnamon and pecans; mix well and sprinkle over pie filling. Drizzle with margarine; microwave on high for 13 minutes. Let stand for 5 minutes; cut into squares.

Patricia Wissler, *Harrisburg, PA*

Country-Style Bread Pudding

This is the best-tasting bread pudding ever, and it's so much easier than making it in the oven.

Makes 8 to 10 servings

3/4 c. brown sugar, packed
8 slices cinnamon-raisin bread, buttered and cubed
4 eggs, beaten
3-1/2 c. milk
1-1/2 t. vanilla extract
Garnish: whipped topping

Sprinkle brown sugar in a slow cooker that has been sprayed with non-stick vegetable spray. Add bread to slow cooker. Whisk together remaining ingredients except whipped cream; pour over bread. Cover and cook on high setting for 2 to 3 hours, until thickened. Do not stir. Spoon pudding into individual bowls. Drizzle brown sugar sauce from slow cooker over pudding. Garnish with dollops of whipped topping.

Tina Wright, *Atlanta, GA*

Simple Skillet Peaches

These peaches are delicious on just about anything you can think of. Cereal, oatmeal, ice cream, cobbler... or use them to top big slices of angel food cake!

Makes about 6 servings

6 c. peaches, peeled, pitted and cut into bite-size pieces
1/2 c. sugar
1 T. vanilla extract

Combine peaches and sugar in a large skillet over medium heat. Bring to a boil; reduce heat to medium-low. Simmer until peaches are soft and mixture has thickened, about 20 to 25 minutes. Stir in extract. Serve warm or chilled.

Nina Roberts, *Queensland, Australia*

Yummy Peach Dessert

A tried & true sweet favorite that everyone loves.

Serves 8 to 10

1/2 c. all-purpose flour
1/2 t. baking soda
1/2 t. salt
1 c. sugar
1 egg, beaten
15-oz. can sliced peaches, drained and chopped
1/2 c. brown sugar, packed
1/4 c. chopped walnuts
Garnish: whipped cream

Sift together flour, baking soda and salt; add sugar. Stir in egg and peaches. Spread in a lightly greased 9"x9" baking pan. Sprinkle with brown sugar and walnuts. Bake at 350 degrees for one hour. Serve warm with whipped cream.

Flavor Booster
·················· ✳ ··················
Cinnamon and nutmeg go great
with peach desserts. Try a little
sprinkle before serving!

Yummy Peach Dessert

Easy Apple Crisp

Nancy Willis, *Farmington Hills, MI*

Easy Apple Crisp

Garnish with a dollop of whipped cream and a dusting of cinnamon.

Serves 12 to 14

4 c. apples, cored and sliced
1/2 c. brown sugar, packed
1/2 c. quick-cooking oats, uncooked
1/3 c. all-purpose flour
3/4 t. cinnamon
1/4 c. margarine

Arrange apple slices in a greased 11"x8" baking pan; set aside. Combine remaining ingredients; stir until crumbly and sprinkle over apples. Bake at 350 degrees for 30 to 35 minutes.

Handy Tip

⋯⋯⋯⋯⋯ ✳ ⋯⋯⋯⋯⋯

Tell someone they're the apple of your eye! Paint a wooden box red, then paint on a cheerful greeting or stencil apples on the outside. Line with a bread cloth and fill with delicious apple crisp or cobbler!

Lynn Filipowicz, *Wilmington, NC*

Pineapple Casserole

I have been making this dish for years…it's good hot or cold.

Serves 8

20-oz. can crushed pineapple
20-oz. can pineapple chunks, drained
2 c. shredded sharp Cheddar cheese
1/4 c. sugar
6 T. all-purpose flour
1 sleeve round buttery crackers, crushed
1/2 c. butter, melted
Optional: pineapple rings, maraschino cherries

Mix together crushed pineapple with juice and remaining ingredients except crackers and butter in a greased 13"x9" baking pan. Top with crackers; drizzle butter over top. Bake, uncovered, at 350 degrees for about 30 minutes, until heated through and bubbly. Garnish with pineapple rings and cherries, if desired.

Brenda Derby, *Northborough, MA*

Apple-Cranberry Crisp

We like to make this using several different varieties of tart baking apples.

Serves 10 to 12

6 c. apples, peeled, cored and sliced
3 c. cranberries
1 c. sugar
2 t. cinnamon
1 to 2 t. lemon juice
3/4 c. butter, sliced and divided
1 c. all-purpose flour
1 c. brown sugar, packed
Garnish: vanilla ice cream

Toss together apple slices, cranberries, sugar and cinnamon. Spread in a buttered 13"x9" glass baking pan. Sprinkle with lemon juice and dot with 1/4 cup butter. Blend remaining butter with flour and brown sugar until crumbly; sprinkle over apple mixture. Bake for one hour at 350 degrees. Serve warm with vanilla ice cream.

Sue Learned, *Wilton, CA*

Perfectly Peachy Cake

This cake is just right to make in the summertime because you don't have to turn on your oven and heat up the kitchen.

Serves 4 to 6

3/4 c. biscuit baking mix
1/2 c. brown sugar, packed
1/3 c. sugar
2 eggs, beaten
2 t. vanilla extract
1/2 c. evaporated milk
2 t. butter, melted
3 peaches, peeled, pitted and mashed
3/4 t. cinnamon
Garnish: vanilla ice cream

In a large bowl, combine baking mix and sugars. Stir in eggs and vanilla until blended. Mix in milk and butter. Fold in peaches and cinnamon until well mixed. Spoon mixture into a lightly greased slow cooker. Cover and cook on low setting for 6 to 8 hours. Serve warm, topped with a scoop of ice cream.

Apple-Cranberry Crisp

Slow-Cooker Caramel Apple Delight

Gretchen Hickman, *Galva, IL*

Crockery Apple Pie

I received this recipe from my great-aunt who owned an orchard. This smells heavenly when it's cooking, and it's perfect served with a big scoop of vanilla bean ice cream.

Serves 10 to 12

6 tart apples, peeled, cored and sliced
2 t. cinnamon
1/4 t. allspice
1/4 t. nutmeg
3/4 c. milk
2 T. butter, softened
3/4 c. sugar
2 eggs, beaten
1 t. vanilla extract
1-1/2 c. biscuit baking mix, divided
1/3 c. brown sugar, packed
3 T. chilled butter

In a large bowl, toss apples with spices. Spoon apple mixture into a lightly greased slow cooker. In a separate bowl, combine milk, softened butter, sugar, eggs, vanilla and 1/2 cup baking mix; stir until well mixed. Spoon batter over apples. Place remaining baking mix and brown sugar in a small bowl. Cut in chilled butter until coarse crumbs form. Sprinkle over batter in slow cooker. Cover and cook on low setting for 6 to 7 hours.

Shelley Turner, *Boise, ID*

Slow-Cooker Caramel Apple Delight

Serve this sweet, gooey delight over vanilla ice cream or slices of angel food cake.

Makes 4 to 6 servings

1/2 c. apple juice
7-oz. pkg. caramels, unwrapped
1 t. vanilla extract
1/2 t. cinnamon
1/3 c. creamy peanut butter
4 to 5 tart apples, peeled, cored and sliced

Combine apple juice, caramels, vanilla and cinnamon in a slow cooker. Add peanut butter; mix well. Add apples; cover and cook on low setting for 5 hours. Stir thoroughly, cover and cook on low setting one additional hour.

Donna Jo Brown, *Peru, IL*

Cherry-Pineapple Dump Cake

Nothing beats this recipe...simply dump in the ingredients, one after another! This cake is a "must" at all Brown family functions.

Serves 8 to 10

14-1/2 oz. can cherry pie filling
20-oz. can chunk pineapple, drained and 1/2 of juice
   reserved
18-1/2 oz. pkg. yellow cake mix
1 t. vanilla extract
1 c. butter, melted
1 c. chopped pecans

Spread pie filling in a greased and floured 13"x9" baking pan; top with pineapple and reserved juice. Stir in dry cake mix and vanilla. Drizzle butter over top; sprinkle with pecans. Bake at 350 degrees for 40 to 45 minutes, until golden.

Gail Hageman, *Albion, ME*

Old-Fashioned Applesauce Cake

Applesauce makes the cake moist and tender.

Makes 8 to 10 servings

2 c. sugar
1/2 c. shortening
2 eggs, beaten
1/2 c. water
1-1/2 c. applesauce
2-1/2 c. all-purpose flour
1-1/2 t. baking soda
1/4 t. baking powder
1-1/2 t. salt
3/4 t. cinnamon
1/2 t. ground cloves
1/2 t. allspice
1/2 c. chopped walnuts

Blend together sugar and shortening; beat in eggs, water and applesauce. Gradually add flour, baking soda, baking powder, salt and spices. Mix thoroughly; stir in nuts. Pour into a greased, floured 13"x9" baking pan. Bake at 350 degrees for one hour, or until cake tests done; watch that edges don't get too dark.

~ *Handy Tip* ~

For an affordable casual get-together, invite friends over for "just desserts!" Offer 2 or 3 simple homebaked desserts like cobblers, dump cake and fruit pie, ice cream for topping and a steamy pot of coffee...they'll love it!

Old-Fashioned Applesauce Cake

Orange-Peach Dump Cake

Elizabeth Wenk, *Cuyahoga Falls, OH*

Orange-Peach Dump Cake

A different flavor combination for this trusty dessert.

Serves 8 to 10

14-1/2 oz. can peach pie filling, chopped
18-oz. pkg. orange cake mix
2 eggs
1/2 c. sour cream

Combine all ingredients in an ungreased 13"x9" baking pan. Mix with a fork until well blended; smooth top. Bake at 350 degrees for 40 to 45 minutes.

Flavor Booster

* * *

Leftover canned pumpkin? Try stirring it into softened vanilla ice cream for a frosty treat.

Darlene Hartzler, *Marshallville, OH*

Pumpkin Cake

My grandma used to make this cake all the time when we were kids. We love it with a little whipped topping.

Serves 8 to 10

15-oz. can pumpkin
1 c. oil
4 eggs
2 c. all-purpose flour
2 c. sugar
1 c. chopped walnuts
2 t. baking soda
2 t. baking powder
2 t. cinnamon
1/2 t. salt

Combine all ingredients; blend well. Pour into a greased 13"x9" baking pan. Bake at 350 degrees for 45 minutes.

Jackie Crough, *Salina, KS*

Hawaiian Cake

Circle the cake plate with a colorful flower lei from a party goods store.

Serves 8 to 10

18-1/4 oz. pkg. white or yellow cake mix
8-oz. pkg. cream cheese, softened
2 c. milk
3.4-oz. pkg. instant vanilla pudding mix
20-oz. can crushed pineapple, drained
16-oz. container frozen whipped topping, thawed
Garnish: toasted coconut, chopped nuts, sliced
    maraschino cherries

Prepare and bake cake mix in a 13"x9" baking pan according to package directions. Let cool. Combine cream cheese, milk and pudding; blend until fluffy. Stir in pineapple. Spread mixture evenly over top of cake; cover with whipped topping. Sprinkle with coconut, nuts and cherries. Chill until serving time.

Dawn Psik, *Aliquippa, PA*

Chocolate Pistachio Dessert

This dessert is sooo light, creamy and tasty! It can be made well ahead of time and refrigerated, so it's perfect for parties.

Makes 15 to 20 servings

3 c. milk
3.4-oz. pkg. instant pistachio pudding mix
3.4-oz. instant white chocolate pudding mix
8-oz. container frozen whipped topping, thawed
14.4-oz. pkg. graham crackers, divided
16-oz. container chocolate frosting

In a large bowl, whisk together milk and pudding mixe for 2 minutes. Let stand for 2 minutes, until softly set. Fold in whipped topping. In an ungreased 13"x9" bakin pan, layer 1/3 of the graham crackers and half the pudding mixture; repeat layers. Top with remaining graham crackers. Refrigerate for at least one hour. Spo frosting into a microwave-safe bowl. Cover and microwave on high for 15 to 20 seconds, until softened stirring once. Spread over dessert. Chill for at least 20 minutes, or until frosting is set.

Hawaiian Cake

Brenda's Fruit Crisp

Kimberly Pfleiderer, *Galion, OH*

Spicy Pumpkin Raisin Cake

An easy-to-make cake that's filled with fall flavors! Tuck a square into family members' lunchboxes for a sweet surprise.

Makes 10 to 12 servings

2 c. all-purpose flour
2 t. baking powder
1 t. baking soda
1/4 t. salt
1 t. cinnamon
1 t. nutmeg
1 t. pumpkin pie spice
1/2 t. ground cloves
2 c. sugar
4 eggs, beaten
1 c. oil
15-oz. can pumpkin
1 c. raisins
16-oz. container cream cheese frosting

In a large bowl, combine all ingredients except frosting. Mix completely. Pour into a greased 13"x9" baking pan. Bake at 350 degrees for 40 to 50 minutes, until a toothpick inserted in center comes out clean. Cool cake before frosting.

Brenda Smith, *Delaware, OH*

Brenda's Fruit Crisp

Here's my favorite dessert recipe...it's a yummy way to use a bumper crop of peaches, apples or berries!

Serves 6

5 c. frozen peaches, apples or berries, thawed and juices reserved
2 to 4 T. sugar
1/2 c. long-cooking oats, uncooked
1/2 c. brown sugar, packed
1/4 c. all-purpose flour
1/4 t. nutmeg
1/4 t. cinnamon
1/4 t. vanilla extract
Optional: 1/4 c. sweetened flaked coconut
1/4 c. butter, diced
Optional: vanilla ice cream

Place fruit and juices in an ungreased 2-quart casserole dish; stir in sugar and set aside. In a medium bowl, mix oats, brown sugar, flour, spices, vanilla and coconut, if using. Add butter to oat mixture; combine until mixture becomes coarse. Sprinkle over fruit. Bake at 375 degrees until golden and tender, 30 to 35 minutes. Serve warm, topped with ice cream if desired.

Lora Montgomery, *Delaware, OH*

Ooey-Gooey Baked Apples

Warm and cozy...yum!

Makes 6 servings

6 Gala or Jonagold apples, cored
1/4 c. butter, softened
1/4 c. brown sugar, packed
1/4 c. maple syrup
1 t. cinnamon
1/2 c. raisins
1/2 c. walnuts, finely chopped
Garnish: 16-oz. jar caramel ice cream topping

Arrange cored apples in a lightly greased 13"x9" baking pan and set aside. Combine butter, brown sugar, maple syrup and cinnamon in a small bowl; stir in raisins and walnuts. Spoon mixture into center of apples; cover with aluminum foil. Bake at 325 degrees for one hour to one hour and 15 minutes, until apples are tender. Serve warm with caramel topping.

Dawn Raskiewicz, *Alliance, NE*

Choco-Mallow Cake

This is my own creation...it's a big hit with my husband!

Makes 8 servings

12-oz. pkg. marshmallows, divided
18-1/4 oz. pkg. yellow cake mix
12-oz. pkg. dark chocolate chips

Place half the marshmallows in a 13"x9" baking pan that has been sprayed with non-stick vegetable spray; set aside. Reserve remaining marshmallows for another recipe. Prepare cake mix according to package directio: Pour batter over marshmallows in the pan. Sprinkle chocolate chips over top of batter. Bake at 350 degrees f 32 to 37 minutes. Marshmallows will rise to top of cake and chocolate chips will sink to bottom.

Flavor Booster

·················· ✳ ··················

Make a nutty dessert topping to spoon over ice cream or sliced pound cake...yum! Mix a cup of toasted walnuts with a cup of maple syrup and place in a jar. Pecans and honey are scrumptious too. The topping may be stored at room temperature up to 2 weeks.

Ooey-Gooey Baked Apples

Fruit & Oat Bars

Mary Alice Dobbert, *King George, VA*

Double Chocolate Brownies

My family's favorite brownies! I love to bake for my family, and these brownies are always a huge success. They travel well too.

Makes 2 dozen

1-1/2 c. all-purpose flour
1 c. baking cocoa
1/2 t. baking powder
1/2 t. salt
2/3 c. butter-flavored shortening
2 c. sugar
4 eggs, beaten
2 c. semi-sweet chocolate chips, divided

Stir together flour, cocoa, baking powder and salt in a bowl; set aside. In a large bowl, combine shortening, sugar and eggs; beat until creamy. Gradually beat in flour mixture. Stir in 1-1/2 cups chocolate chips. Pour batter into a greased 13"x9" baking pan. Bake at 350 degrees for 25 to 30 minutes, until a toothpick inserted in the center comes out clean. Sprinkle remaining chips on top. Let stand 5 minutes, until chips melt; spread with a spatula to frost brownies. Cool completely in pan on a wire rack. Cut into squares.

Leslie Harvie, *Simpsonville, SC*

Fruit & Oat Bars

When I was a child, my mother would whip up a batch of these yummy bars every Saturday morning. Strawberry was my favorite flavor!

Makes 1-1/2 dozen

15-1/4 oz. pkg. yellow cake mix
2-1/2 c. quick-cooking oats, uncooked
3/4 c. butter, melted
12-oz. jar favorite-flavor jam or preserves
1 T. water

In a large bowl, combine dry cake mix and oats. Add melted butter; mix until crumbly. Add half of crumb mixture to a greased 13"x9" baking pan; press firmly to cover bottom of pan. Stir together jam or preserves and water; spoon over layer in pan. Cover with remaining crumb mixture. Pat firmly to form an even layer. Bake at 375 degrees for 20 minutes. Cool and cut into bars.

Donna Elliott, *Winchester, TN*

Cup of Cobbler

My simple fruit cobbler recipe tastes as good as my granny's!

Serves 4 to 6

1/2 c. butter, sliced
1 c. all-purpose flour
1 c. sugar
1 c. milk
15-oz. can sliced peaches, cherries or blackberries in syrup

Add butter to a lightly greased one-quart casserole dish; melt in a 350-degree oven. In a bowl, stir together flour, sugar and milk; pour batter into melted butter. Pour undrained fruit over top; do not stir. Bake at 350 degrees for 30 to 40 minutes, until bubbly and golden. Serve warm.

Arlene Smulski, *Lyons, IL*

Chocolate-Cherry Cobbler

Top with dollops of whipped cream...luscious!

Makes 4 to 6 servings

1/4 c. butter, melted
1/2 t. vanilla extract
30-oz. can cherry pie filling
1 c. all-purpose flour
1 c. sugar
1-1/2 t. baking powder
1/4 c. baking cocoa
1/2 c. milk

In a small bowl, combine melted butter and vanilla; spread mixture in a 13"x9" baking pan. Pour pie filling into pan; set aside. In a bowl, mix together flour, sugar, baking powder and cocoa. Stir in milk. Pour batter over pie filling; do not stir. Bake at 350 degrees for 30 to 40 minutes, until golden. Serve warm.

~ Handy Tip ~
Most fruit pies and cobblers can be frozen for as long as 4 months...what a time-saver! Cool completely after baking, then wrap well in plastic wrap and 2 layers of aluminum foil before freezing. To serve, thaw overnight in the refrigerator, bring to room temperature and rewarm in the oven.

Cup of Cobbler

Index

Index

U. S. to Metric Recipe Equivalents

Volume Measurements

¼ teaspoon .... 1 mL
½ teaspoon .... 2 mL
1 teaspoon .... 5 mL
1 tablespoon = 3 teaspoons .... 15 mL
2 tablespoons = 1 fluid ounce .... 30 mL
¼ cup .... 60 mL
⅓ cup .... 75 mL
½ cup = 4 fluid ounces .... 125 mL
1 cup = 8 fluid ounces .... 250 mL
2 cups = 1 pint = 16 fluid ounces .. 500 mL
4 cups = 1 quart .... 1 L

Weights

1 ounce .... 30 g
4 ounces .... 120 g
8 ounces .... 225 g
16 ounces = 1 pound .... 450 g

Baking Pan Sizes

Square
8x8x2 inches .... 2 L = 20x20x5 cm
9x9x2 inches .... 2.5 L = 23x23x5 cm

Rectangular
13x9x2 inches .... 3.5 L = 33x23x5 cm

Loaf
9x5x3 inches .... 2 L = 23x13x7 cm

Round
8x1-1/2 inches .... 1.2 L = 20x4 cm
9x1-1/2 inches .... 1.5 L = 23x4 cm

Recipe Abbreviations

t. = teaspoon   ltr. = liter
T. = tablespoon   oz. = ounce
c. = cup   lb. = pound
pt. = pint   doz. = dozen
qt. = quart   pkg. = package
gal. = gallon   env. = envelope

Oven Temperatures

300˚ F .... 150° C
325˚ F .... 160° C
350˚ F .... 180° C
375˚ F .... 190° C
400˚ F .... 200° C
450˚ F .... 230° C

Kitchen Measurements

A pinch = ⅛ teaspoon
1 fluid ounce = 2 tablespoons
3 teaspoons = 1 tablespoon
4 fluid ounces = ½ cup
2 tablespoons = ⅛ cup
8 fluid ounces = 1 cup
4 tablespoons = ¼ cup
16 fluid ounces = 1 pint
8 tablespoons = ½ cup
32 fluid ounces = 1 quart
16 tablespoons = 1 cup
16 ounces net weight = 1 pound
2 cups = 1 pint
4 cups = 1 quart
4 quarts = 1 gallon

Send us your favorite recipe

and the memory that makes it special for you!*

If we select your recipe for a brand-new **Gooseberry Patch** cookbook, your name will appear right along with it...and you'll receive a FREE copy of the book!

Submit your recipe on our website at
www.gooseberrypatch.com/sharearecipe

*Please include the number of servings and all other necessary information.

Have a taste for more?

Visit www.gooseberrypatch.com to join our Circle of Friends!

- Free recipes, tips and ideas plus a complete cookbook index
- Get mouthwatering recipes and special email offers delivered to your inbox

You'll also love these cookbooks from **Gooseberry Patch**!

150 Best-Ever Cast-Iron Skillet Recipes

150 Recipes In a 13x9 Pan

5-Ingredient Family Favorite Recipes

America's Comfort Foods

Best Church Suppers

Busy-Day Slow Cooking

Christmas Comfort Classics

Delicious Recipes for Diabetics

From Grandma's Kitchen

Homestyle in a Hurry

Meals in Minutes: 15, 20, 30 Minutes

Sunday Dinner At Grandma's

Tasty Fall Cooking

Weeknight Dinners 6 Ingredients Or Less

www.gooseberrypatch.com